P · E · R · F · E · C

FRENCh
COUNTRY COOKING

CW00324017

P·E·R·F·E·C·T
FRENCH
COUNTRY COOKING

DORLING KINDERSLEY
LONDON • NEW YORK • SYDNEY • MOSCOW

A DORLING KINDERSLEY BOOK

Created and Produced by
CARROLL & BROWN LIMITED
5 Lonsdale Road
London NW6 6RA

Project Editor Anne Crane
Assistant Editors Valerie Cipollone and Stella Vayne

Editorial Consultant Jeni Wright

Art Editor Alan Watt
Designers Sue Knight and Lucy De Rosa

Photographers David Murray and Jules Selmes

Production Wendy Rogers and Amanda Mackie

First published in Great Britain in 1997
by Dorling Kindersley Limited
9 Henrietta Street, London WC2E 8PS

Previously published in 1995 under the title
Look & Cook French Country Cooking.

Copyright © 1995, 1997 Dorling Kindersley Limited
Text copyright © 1995, 1997 Anne Willan Inc.

Visit us on the World Wide Web at http://www.dk.com

All rights reserved. No part of this publication may be
reproduced, stored in a retrieval system, or transmitted in
any form or by any means, electronic, mechanical, photocopying,
recording, or otherwise, without the prior written permission
of the copyright owner.

A CIP catalogue record for this book is available
from the British Library

ISBN 0-7513-0491-3

Reproduced by Colourscan, Singapore
Printed and bound in Singapore by Star Standard

CONTENTS

PERFECT FRENCH COUNTRY COOKING

Welcome to **Perfect French Country** Cooking. This volume is designed to be the simplest, most informative cookbook you'll ever own. It is the closest I can come to sharing my personal techniques for cooking my favourite recipes without actually being with you in the kitchen.

Equipment and ingredients often determine whether or not you can cook a particular dish, so **Perfect French Country Cooking** illustrates everything you need at the beginning of each recipe. You'll see at a glance how long a recipe takes to cook, how many servings it makes, what the finished dish looks like, and how much preparation can be done ahead. When you start to cook, you will find that the preparation and cooking are organized into easy-to-follow steps. Each stage has its own colour coding, and every-thing is shown in photographs with brief text accompanying each step. You will never be in doubt as to what it is you are doing, why you are doing it, or how it should look.

EQUIPMENT

INGREDIENTS

🍲 SERVES 4–6 🥣 WORK TIME 25–35 MINUTES 🍲 COOKING TIME 20–30 MINUTES

I've also included helpful hints and ideas under "Anne Says". These may list an alternative ingredient or piece of equipment, or explain the reason for using a certain method, or offer advice on mastering a particular technique. Similarly, if there is a crucial stage in a recipe when things can go wrong, I've included some warnings called "Take Care".

Many of the photographs are annotated to pinpoint why a certain piece of equipment works best, or how food should look at that stage of cooking. Because presentation is so important, there is a picture of the finished dish at the end of each recipe, often with serving suggestions.

Thanks to all this information, you can't go wrong. I'll be with you every step of the way. So please come with me into the kitchen to look, cook, and create some delicious recipes from **Perfect French Country Cooking**.

WHY FRENCH COUNTRY COOKING?

French country cooking survives triumphantly despite the vagaries of fashion. The combination of top-quality ingredients and traditional recipes has proved unbeatable time and time again. Consider cassoulet: *pungent Languedoc sausage and garlic, plus the inspired addition of duck confit, transforms what would otherwise be little more than a pot of pork and baked beans. The humble bacon and egg pie,* quiche Lorraine, *has achieved world renown simply because French cooks insist on using full-flavoured smoky bacon in the rich custard, and on prebaking the pastry shell so that it remains crisp. It is this attention to ingredients and technique that gives French country cooking its authority.*

Even today, France can still lay claim to the world's finest ingredients. The Paris basin has long been known as France's bread basket, while on the fertile soil of Burgundy to the south and the Loire to the west there are orchards and market gardens, pedigree beef cattle such as Charolais, and free-range chickens like those of Bresse, the aristocrats of the farmyard. Quality control of food began in France with the appellation controlée *status for wines, a concept which has since been extended to a range of foods, notably poultry and cheese.*

Brittany and the northern coastline offer superb fish and shellfish. In the south, the Mediterranean still furnishes specialities like spiny lobster and red mullet. Inland, especially in the mountains, there are dried hams and sausages, and fine cheeses.

In making the most of this material, simplicity is the key. Solo ingredients are orchestrated with vegetables, herbs, butter or oil, and wine or cider. Natural marriages abound. You find the small hens that live among the vines are cooked with vine leaves, while Gascon prunes marinated in local Armagnac form the basis of a sublime ice cream. Long slow simmering in a braise, soup, or stew is characteristic, and where would the French kitchen be without the stockpot?

As everywhere else, cooking is changing in rural France. The microwaved hamburger and the packaged pizza can now be found in the smallest village café. But that same village will have a baker who rises at 4 o'clock in the morning, six days a week, to produce crusty loaves for the breakfast table. In all but the largest cities, lunch remains the main meal of the day to be shared with the whole family, and three, even four, courses are routine. Supper holds true to its original meaning of soup, with perhaps an omelette or a slice of ham, and plenty of bread. Grand desserts, such as snow eggs, are reserved for weekends and feast days, as are the great classics of country cooking, such as duck with tart cherries. These are savoured at leisure around the family table. You'll find a few of them in this book, together with a warming collection of the more everyday dishes that country cooks do so well. I hope you enjoy them all as much as I do.

RECIPE CHOICE

A French cook shops regularly at the local market, and plans the meal around the produce available. I like to do the same, preparing hearty meals laden with root vegetables in the winter, and serving tender vegetables, lighter greens, and salads as the weather warms in spring. In summer, choose recipes abundant in aromatic herbs and fresh fruit. Below is a summary of recipes you will find in this volume.

FIRST COURSES

Black Olive Dip with Crudités (La Grande Tapenade): a platter of crisp fresh vegetables is served with a pungent sauce of black olives puréed with capers, anchovies, and garlic. *Eggs Stuffed with Black Olive and Anchovy Sauce (Oeufs Durs en Tapenade)*: the olive sauce is mellowed with the addition of hard-boiled egg yolks, then piped into egg-white halves. *Warm Salad of Wild Mushrooms (Salade Tiède aux Champignons Sauvages)*: sautéed fresh wild mushrooms are set off with a salad of gourmet greens. *Warm Salad of Chicken Livers (Salade Tiède aux Foies de Volaille)*: pieces of sautéed chicken liver are teamed with gourmet salad greens. *Country Terrine (Terrine de Campagne)*: slices of this terrine reveal strips of ham running through a traditional forcemeat mixture of minced pork and veal flavoured with brandy and spices. *Game Terrine (Terrine de Gibier)*: for an autumnal version of Country Terrine, minced venison replaces the veal.

MAIN DISHES AND ACCOMPANIMENTS

Quiche Lorraine: I like to add Gruyère cheese to this French classic of egg custard and bacon in a flaky pastry shell. *Leek and Cheese Quiche (Quiche aux Poireaux et Fromage)*: sliced leeks are cooked until soft, then baked in the egg custard with plenty of Gruyère cheese. *Buckwheat Crêpes with Seafood (Galettes de Sarrasin aux Fruits de Mer)*: nutty buckwheat crêpes are rolled around a creamy seafood mixture of prawns, scallops, and sole. *Buckwheat Crêpes with Ham (Galettes de Sarrasin au Jambon)*:

the French version of a ham and cheese sandwich. *Omelette with Peppers and Tomatoes (Omelette Basquaise)*: a zesty combination of red peppers, onions, and tomatoes, spiked with hot red chillies, fills this flat omelette from southwestern France. *Country Omelette (Omelette Paysanne)*: cubes of potatoes, crisp bacon, and sliced onions are the filling for this tasty omelette. *Scallops with Tomatoes, Garlic, and Herbs (Coquilles St Jacques à la Provençale)*: sweet scallops are briskly cooked, then paired with a tomato and garlic *concassée*. *Spiced Scallops (Coquilles St Jacques Nantaise)*: Nantes, once the spice port for the Orient, boasts this recipe of scallops flavoured with curry spices, tomatoes, and onion. *Roast Sea Bass with Herb Butter Sauce (Loup Rôti au Beurre de Montpellier)*: sliced lemon and sprigs of fresh thyme stud a whole roasted sea bass. A Mediterranean combination of olive oil, anchovies, capers, garlic, and herbs features in the accompanying sauce. *Loire Sea Bass (Loup Rôti, Sauce Beurre Blanc)*: slightly acidic *beurre blanc* is the perfect balance to the mild roast sea bass. *Sweet-Sour Duck with Cherries (Canard aux Cerises à l'Aigre-doux)*: tangy cherries are the ideal foil to the rich flavour of crisp roast duck. *Duck with Pears (Canard aux Poires)*: roast duck is teamed with pear halves poached in red wine. *Poussins in Vine Leaves (Coquelets à la Vigneronne)*: stuffed small chickens keep moist when wrapped in vine leaves and rashers of bacon. *Poussins with Braised Chicory (Coquelets aux Endives Braisées)*: braised chicory accompanies stuffed small chickens served with a sharp vinegar sauce. *Sauté of Chicken with Prawns (Sauté de Poulet aux Crevettes)*: chicken and prawns marry in this sauté from Burgundy. Tomatoes, white wine, chicken stock, and a splash of *marc de Bourgogne* add characteristic flavour. *Sauté of Chicken with Fennel (Sauté de Poulet au Fenouil)*: the aniseed flavour of fennel blends pleasantly with chicken as they cook together in this sauté. *Rabbit with Provençal Herbs and Baked Tomatoes (Lapin aux Herbes de Provence, Tomates au Four)*: a marinade of Provençal herbs, olive oil, and white wine doubles as the cooking liquid in this rabbit stew. Plum tomatoes are slowly baked until sweet and tender to serve as an accompaniment. *Chicken with Provençal Herbs and Garlic Potatoes (Poulet aux Herbes de Provence, Pommes à l'Ail)*: chicken replaces the rabbit in this stew served with crisp garlic-flavoured potatoes. *Cassoulet with Quick Confit*: a hearty winter casserole – speedy duck confit, cubes of lamb, and pork sausage are stewed with beans and tomatoes and topped with a golden crust. *Poor Man's Cassoulet*: cubes of pork replace the lamb in this simpler version of cassoulet. *Spring Lamb Stew (Navarin Printanier)*: in this distinctive stew, chunks of lamb are simmered in stock until just tender, then cooked with carrots, turnips, potatoes, baby onions, green beans, and peas. *Lamb Ratatouille (Ratatouille d'Agneau)*: green and red pepper strips, aubergines, tomatoes, and onions form a ratatouille before combining with the lamb in this succulent stew. *Leg of Lamb with Roasted Garlic and Shallots (Gigot à l'Ail et aux Echalotes Rôtis)*: garlic cloves and whole shallots mellow and sweeten when they are roasted beside a leg of lamb. *Leg of Lamb with Potatoes (Gigot Boulangère)*: sliced potatoes and onion roast beneath a leg of lamb and absorb the tasty cooking juices. *Steak au Poivre*: crushed black peppercorns add heat to steak, and French fried potatoes are the perfect accompaniment. *Steak with White Wine and Shallots (Steak au Vin Blanc et Echalotes)*: individual steaks feature in this version of Steak au Poivre served with an intensely flavoured white wine sauce and crunchy French fried potatoes. *Pork Chops with Mustard Sauce (Côtes de Porc Dijonnaise)*: a lively mustard sauce highlights tender pork chops. *Veal Chops with Mustard Sauce and Baby Onions (Côtes de Veau Dijonnaise aux Petits Oignons)*: the mustard sauce complements the mild flavour of veal with baby onions. *Courgette Tian (Tian de Courgettes)*: in this Provençal speciality, chopped courgettes, garlic, and onion are baked with cooked rice and eggs. *Spinach and Mushroom Tian (Tian d'Epinards et Champignons)*: a tempting side dish of spinach and mushrooms flavoured with grated Parmesan. *Gratin Dauphinois*: thinly sliced potatoes, cooked first in milk, then in double cream, are sprinkled with Gruyère cheese, and baked until bubbling – a rich and delicious accompaniment to any meal. *Gratin of Root Vegetables (Gratin de Racines d'Hiver)*: carrots brighten this rich version of Gratin Dauphinois.

DESSERTS

Cherry Clafoutis (Clafoutis aux Cerises): fresh cherries stud a baked batter pudding that is dusted with icing sugar just before serving. *Plum Clafoutis (Clafoutis aux Prunes)*: purple plum halves are baked in batter. *Apricot and Hazelnut Ice Cream (Glace Auxerroise)*: dried apricots enhance the flavour, while chopped hazelnuts add crunch to vanilla ice cream. *Prune and Armagnac Ice Cream (Glace Gasconne)*: a Gascon favourite – vanilla ice cream is flecked with Armagnac-soaked prunes. *Golden Rice Pudding with Peaches and Red Wine (Terrinée et Chicolle)*: fresh peaches macerated in red wine add an appealing contrast to this creamy rice pudding. *Rice Pudding with Dried Fruit Compote (Terrinée à la Confit de Fruits Secs)*: dried figs, apricots, and sultanas are cooked with a clove to serve with a soft rice pudding. *Snow Eggs (Oeufs à la Neige)*: a caramel lattice decorates clouds of meringue floating on a pool of vanilla custard sauce. *Chocolate Snow Eggs (Oeufs à la Neige au Chocolat)*: plain chocolate darkens the custard sauce and decorates the meringues. *Rustic Apple Tart (Tarte aux Pommes Ménagère)*: an apple purée hides beneath a fan of apple slices in a pastry crust. *Apple Tartlets (Tartelettes aux Pommes)*: an elegant version of a classic dessert.

FRENCH COUNTRY MENUS

French country dining is often based on family meals. The midday meal, traditionally the day's largest, is usually served in several courses. It may open with a slice of pâté, slivers of dried sausage, or perhaps a salad of grated carrot. The main course will be chicken or meat, fish on Fridays, with a vegetable, followed by cheese, then fruit. The evening meal is much simpler, usually just one course.

Seasons and special occasions figure in menu planning as well. Summer is the season for lighter meals. For a casual evening among friends, Black Olive Dip with Crudités as an opener, and Roast Sea Bass with Herb Butter Sauce as a main course are both easy to prepare. Finish the meal with French cheeses and fresh fruit.

Plan an elegant dinner to show off autumn produce, and begin the meal with Warm Salad of Wild Mushrooms. Serve Poussins in Vine Leaves to celebrate the grape harvest, followed by freshly baked Apple Tartlets, all accompanied by your favourite French wine, red or white.

Holiday meals deserve special attention as well as special ingredients. Start the meal with Scallops with Tomatoes, Garlic, and Herbs. The tomato garnish may be prepared in advance, but cook the scallops just before serving. Leg of Lamb with Roasted Garlic and Shallots warrants an equally distinctive accompaniment, like Courgette Tian. For dessert, impress your family and friends with Snow Eggs floating in vanilla custard, topped with a golden caramel lattice and flaked almonds.

BLACK OLIVE DIP WITH CRUDITES

La Grande Tapenade

EQUIPMENT

chef's knife

small knife

vegetable peeler

food processor

olive stoner

bowls

rubber spatula

serrated knife

baking sheet

chopping board

The Provençal sauce, tapenade, *combines the quintessential flavours of the Mediterranean – black olives, olive oil, anchovy, garlic, and capers. It is most often served with crudités.*

GETTING AHEAD

The sauce can be made up to 1 week ahead. Pour a thin layer of olive oil over the top, and keep it, tightly covered, in the refrigerator. The vegetables can be prepared, wrapped in damp paper towels, and refrigerated up to 8 hours ahead.

metric	SHOPPING LIST	imperial
1	medium bunch of spring onions	1
1	red pepper	1
1	green pepper	1
1	medium cucumber	1
1	medium bunch of radishes	1
1	French baguette	1
250 g	cherry tomatoes	8 oz
	For the tapenade	
4	garlic cloves	4
200 g	oil-cured black olives	6 1/2 oz
6	slices of white bread	6
30 g	drained capers	1 oz
6	anchovy fillets	6
125 ml	olive oil	4 fl oz
	lemon juice to taste	
	pepper	

INGREDIENTS

oil-cured black olives

white bread

anchovy fillets

garlic cloves

capers

spring onions

cucumber

red pepper

radishes

olive oil

cherry tomatoes

lemon juice

green pepper

French baguette

ORDER OF WORK

1   **MAKE THE TAPENADE**

2   **PREPARE THE VEGETABLES AND ASSEMBLE THE DISH**

1 MAKE THE TAPENADE

If available, buy oil-cured black olives from Provence

Olive stoner makes removing stones easy

1 Set the flat side of the chef's knife on top of each garlic clove and strike it with your fist. Discard the skin.

2 Using the olive stoner, stone the olives and discard the stones.

3 With the serrated knife, trim and discard the crusts from the bread. Roughly tear the bread slices into pieces and place them in a medium bowl. Pour cold water over the slices to generously cover them. Leave to soak, 5 minutes.

4 Squeeze the bread dry with your fists and put the pieces into the food processor.

Olive oil is added in steady stream

5 Add the garlic cloves, olives, capers, and anchovy fillets to the food processor and chop coarsely. With the blades turning, gradually add the olive oil. Add lemon juice and pepper to taste, and work again briefly.

6 Transfer the tapenade to a bowl, scraping the side of the processor bowl with the rubber spatula. Cover, and set aside until ready to serve.

ANNE SAYS
"You can make a coarse or finely chopped mixture, as you prefer."

HOW TO CORE AND SEED A PEPPER AND CUT IT INTO STRIPS OR DICE

The core and seeds of a pepper should be discarded before cutting the pepper into strips or dice.

1 With a small knife, cut around the core of the pepper. Twist the core, and pull it out.

2 Halve the pepper lengthways, and scrape out the seeds. Cut away the white ribs on the inside.

3 Set each pepper half cut-side down, flatten it with the heel of your hand, and, using a chef's knife, slice it lengthways into strips. For dice, gather the strips together, and cut crossways.

2 PREPARE THE VEGETABLES AND ASSEMBLE THE DISH

1 Trim the spring onions and cut them into 5 cm (2 inch) pieces, including some of their green tops. Core and seed the peppers and cut them into strips (see box, left).

2 Trim the ends off the cucumber with the chef's knife, then peel it with the vegetable peeler.

Cucumber seeds are discarded

3 Cut the cucumber in half lengthways, then scoop out the seeds with a teaspoon.

4 Cut each cucumber half into 2–3 strips lengthways, then gather the strips into a bundle and cut them crossways into 5 cm (2 inch) pieces.

5 Using the small knife, trim the roots and tops of the radishes, leaving a little of the stalks.

After baking, bread should feel crisp

1 Heat the oven to 190°C (375°F, Gas 5). With the serrated knife, cut the bread into 5 mm (1/4 inch) slices on the diagonal, discarding the ends. Set the slices on the baking sheet and bake in the heated oven until crisp and beginning to brown, 10–15 minutes.

🍽 TO SERVE

Transfer the tapenade to a small serving bowl and set it in the centre of a large platter. Arrange the spring onions, radishes, cucumber strips, pepper strips, and cherry tomatoes around the tapenade. Serve the toasted bread separately.

Tapenade is delicious accompaniment to aperitifs

Crisp bread and crudités both go well with tapenade

EGGS STUFFED WITH BLACK OLIVE AND ANCHOVY SAUCE

OEUFS DURS EN TAPENADE

In this Provençal version of devilled eggs, the yolks of hard-boiled eggs are blended with the tapenade mixture. The sauce can be made up to 1 week ahead, but cook the eggs the day of serving.

1 Omit the spring onions, peppers, cucumber, radishes, French baguette, and cherry tomatoes. Make the tapenade as directed, omitting the bread and using 3 garlic cloves, 100 g (3 1/2 oz) oil-cured black olives, 4 anchovy fillets, 30 ml (2 tbsp) drained capers, 75 ml (2 1/2 fl oz) olive oil, and pepper to taste. Cut 4 more anchovy fillets lengthways in half, then cut each half crossways into 3 pieces and set them aside for decoration.

2 Put 6 eggs into a saucepan of cold water, bring to a boil, and simmer, 10 minutes. Remove from the heat and run cold water into the pan to stop the eggs cooking. Allow to cool, then drain. Tap the eggs to crack the shells, then peel them, rinse with cold water, and pat dry.

3 Slice the eggs lengthways in half, then separate the yolks from the whites. Put the yolks into a sieve set over a medium bowl and work them through with the back of a metal spoon. Scrape away the yolk clinging to the bottom of the sieve. Reserve 30 ml (2 tbsp) of the yolks for decoration, add the tapenade to the remaining yolks, and beat with a wooden spoon until well mixed.

4 Shortly before serving, stuff the egg whites: put the tapenade mixture into a piping bag fitted with a large star tube and pipe rosettes into the egg whites. Alternatively, use a teaspoon to fill the egg whites. Top each half with a little sieved egg yolk and an anchovy cross. Arrange the stuffed eggs on a platter and decorate with parsley sprigs. Serves 4–6.

WARM SALAD OF WILD MUSHROOMS

Salade Tiède aux Champignons Sauvages

 SERVES 4   WORK TIME 25–30 MINUTES   COOKING TIME 8–10 MINUTES

EQUIPMENT

chef's knife

wooden spoon

small knife

large frying pan

whisk

bowls

salad spinner†

chopping board

paper towels

Wild mushrooms are a true delicacy calling for the simplest preparation. A favourite first course is to sauté the mushrooms with chopped shallot and parsley and serve them on a bed of salad.

GETTING AHEAD
The vinaigrette dressing can be made up to 1 week in advance and kept in a sealed container. Prepare the salad leaves up to 1 day ahead and keep them, wrapped in a tea towel, in the refrigerator.

metric	SHOPPING LIST	imperial
1	small head of frisée, weighing about 125 g (4 oz)	1
1	small head of radicchio, weighing about 75 g (2½ oz)	1
75 g	rocket	2½ oz
375 g	mixed wild mushrooms, such as chanterelles, oyster mushrooms, and cèpes	12 oz
2	shallots	2
1	small bunch of parsley	1
30–45 g	butter	1–1½ oz
	For the vinaigrette dressing	
30 ml	red wine vinegar	2 tbsp
2.5 ml	Dijon mustard	½ tsp
	salt and pepper	
45 ml	vegetable oil	3 tbsp
45 ml	walnut oil	3 tbsp

†tea towel can also be used

INGREDIENTS

vegetable oil

mixed wild mushrooms

red wine vinegar

radicchio

rocket

butter

parsley

walnut oil

shallots

Dijon mustard

frisée

ANNE SAYS
"To make expensive wild mushrooms go further, you can replace half of them with button mushrooms."

ORDER OF WORK

1 MAKE THE VINAIGRETTE DRESSING AND WASH THE GREENS

2 PREPARE THE MUSHROOMS AND ASSEMBLE THE SALAD

1 MAKE THE VINAIGRETTE DRESSING AND WASH THE GREENS

1 Make the vinaigrette dressing (see box, below). Pull the frisée leaves apart and discard the tough stalks. Tear the leaves into pieces and immerse them in plenty of cold water.

All salad leaves are washed together

2 Discard any withered outer leaves from the radicchio and cut away the core. Separate the leaves and immerse them with the frisée pieces.

3 Discard the tough stalks from the rocket and immerse the leaves in the bowl of cold water.

Tough stalks are removed before leaves are washed

4 Wash the frisée, radicchio, and rocket leaves thoroughly. Dry the leaves in the salad spinner or on a tea towel, then transfer all the leaves to a large bowl.

HOW TO MAKE VINAIGRETTE DRESSING

The standard recipe for vinaigrette dressing follows the principle of 1 part vinegar to 3 parts oil, but these quantities can vary according to taste, the type of vinegar and oil, and the other ingredients used.

In a bowl, whisk together the vinegar, mustard, and salt and pepper. Gradually whisk in the vegetable and walnut oils so the vinaigrette emulsifies and thickens slightly. Taste for seasoning.

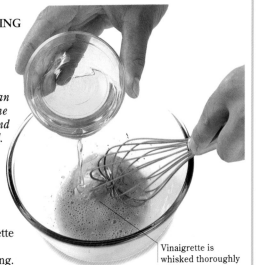

Vinaigrette is whisked thoroughly

2 PREPARE THE MUSHROOMS AND ASSEMBLE THE SALAD

1 Wipe the wild mushrooms with damp paper towels. Wash them only if they are very dirty, and do not let them soak in water. Trim the stalks and remove woody portions.

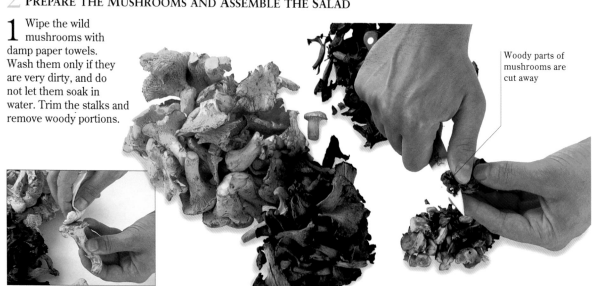

Woody parts of mushrooms are cut away

2 Place the mushrooms on a chopping board and cut them into medium pieces with the chef's knife.

3 Peel the shallots, leaving a little of the root attached, and cut them in half. Set each half, flat-side down, on the chopping board and slice horizontally, leaving the slices attached at the root. Slice vertically, again leaving the root end uncut, then cut across the shallot to make fine dice.

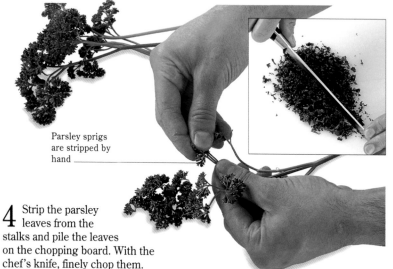

Parsley sprigs are stripped by hand

4 Strip the parsley leaves from the stalks and pile the leaves on the chopping board. With the chef's knife, finely chop them.

5 Heat the butter in the frying pan until foaming. Add the shallots and cook, stirring occasionally, until soft, 2–3 minutes.

6 Add the mushrooms and salt and pepper. Cook, stirring, until the mushrooms are tender and all the liquid has evaporated, 5–7 minutes. Stir in the chopped parsley and taste for seasoning.

Parsley is added when mushrooms are almost cooked

7 Briskly whisk the vinaigrette to re-emulsify it, then pour it over the salad leaves and toss them until coated. Taste for seasoning.

! TAKE CARE !
If the salad leaves are tossed in the vinaigrette too far in advance they will wilt.

¶◎¶ TO SERVE
Divide the salad leaves among 4 individual plates. Spoon over the mushrooms. Serve at once, while the salad leaves are crisp and the mushrooms still warm.

Wild mushrooms have exceptional flavour

Salad leaves can be varied according to taste

VARIATION
WARM SALAD OF CHICKEN LIVERS
SALADE TIEDE AUX FOIES DE VOLAILLE

Chicken livers, cooked with a touch of red wine vinegar, take the place of wild mushrooms in this bistro-style salad.

1 Omit the wild mushrooms and parsley. Make the vinaigrette dressing and prepare the salad leaves as directed. Using a small knife, trim any membrane from 4 chicken livers (total weight about 125 g/4 oz), then cut each liver into 3 pieces. Coarsely chop the leaves from 5–7 sprigs of fresh tarragon.
2 Toss the salad leaves in the vinaigrette dressing, then arrange them on 4 individual plates.
3 Melt 30 g (1 oz) butter in a frying pan, add the shallots, and sauté until soft. Add the chicken livers and salt and pepper. Fry the livers over high heat, shaking the pan occasionally, until they are brown on the outside, 1–2 minutes.
4 Add 30 ml (2 tbsp) red wine vinegar and bring to a boil, stirring to dissolve the pan juices. Stir in the chopped tarragon. Spoon 3 pieces of chicken liver with some pan juices onto each plate of salad. Serve at once.

COUNTRY TERRINE

Terrine de Campagne

 SERVES 8–10   WORK TIME 35–40 MINUTES*   COOKING TIME 1¼–1½ HOURS

EQUIPMENT

terrine with lid
(30 x 7.5 x 7.5 cm/
12 x 3 x 3 inches)

medium
frying pan

roasting tin

paper towels

bowls

chef's knife

palette knife

medium
saucepan

large metal spoon

wooden spoon

sieve

small knife

metal skewer

chopping board

Country terrines are rich mixtures of meat, either coarsely chopped or smooth. The meat can be used alone, or layered with strips of game, liver, veal, or ham, often interleaved with pork fat for richness.

GETTING AHEAD

Country terrine can be made up to 5 days ahead and kept, covered, in the refrigerator; the flavours will mellow.

*plus 1 hour marinating and 24 hours chilling time

metric	SHOPPING LIST	imperial
1	thick slice cooked ham, weighing about 125 g (4 oz)	1
30 ml	brandy	2 tbsp
1	medium onion	1
2–3	sprigs of fresh thyme	2–3
2	garlic cloves	2
125 g	chicken livers	4 oz
15 g	butter	½ oz
625 g	minced pork, part fat, part lean	1¼ lb
250 g	minced veal	8 oz
1.25 ml	ground allspice	¼ tsp
1	pinch of ground nutmeg	1
1	pinch of ground cloves	1
2	eggs	2
1	bay leaf	1
	salt and pepper	
8–10	gherkins	8–10
For lining and sealing the terrine		
250 g	barding fat	8 oz
45 g	plain flour	1½ oz
30–45 ml	water	2–3 tbsp

INGREDIENTS

cooked
ham

chicken
livers

minced
veal

minced
pork

eggs

barding
fat

gherkins

brandy

ground
nutmeg

ground
allspice

garlic cloves

onion

ground
cloves

fresh thyme

butter

bay leaf

plain flour

ANNE SAYS

"Barding fat is thinly sliced pork fat, available at specialist butchers. You can use sliced fat bacon instead."

ORDER OF WORK

1 PREPARE THE
INGREDIENTS

2 ASSEMBLE AND
BAKE THE TERRINE

3 FINISH THE
TERRINE

1 PREPARE THE INGREDIENTS

1 Place the slice of cooked ham on the chopping board and, using the chef's knife, slice it into long strips about 1 cm (3/8 inch) wide.

2 Combine the ham, brandy, and salt and pepper in a bowl. Cover, and let marinate, 1 hour. Meanwhile, prepare the remaining ingredients.

3 Peel the onion, leaving a little of the root attached and cut it lengthways in half. Lay each onion half flat on the chopping board and slice horizontally towards the root, leaving the slices attached at the root end. Then slice vertically, again leaving the root end uncut. Finally, cut across the onion to make dice. Continue chopping the onion until it is very fine.

4 Strip the thyme leaves from the stalks. Peel and finely chop the garlic cloves (see box, right). Trim any membrane from the chicken livers, and coarsely chop them.

Chicken liver adds rich flavour to terrine

HOW TO PEEL AND CHOP GARLIC

The strength of garlic varies with its age and dryness; use more when it is very fresh.

1 To separate the cloves, crush the bulb with the heel of your hand or pull a clove from the bulb with your fingers. To peel the clove, lightly crush it with the flat side of a chef's knife to loosen the skin.

2 Peel the skin from the garlic clove with your fingers.

3 To crush the clove, set the flat side of the knife on top and strike firmly with your fist. Finely chop the garlic with the knife, rocking the blade back and forth.

5 Melt the butter in the frying pan, add the onion, and cook, stirring occasionally, until soft and brown, 3–5 minutes. Turn into a bowl; let cool.

6 Add the garlic, thyme, chicken livers, minced pork, minced veal, allspice, nutmeg, cloves, and salt and pepper. Mix with a wooden spoon.

7 Crack the eggs into a bowl. Using a fork, beat the eggs to mix, then add them to the meat mixture.

Ham strips are flavoured with brandy marinade

Mixture is combination of pork, veal, herbs, and spices

8 Strain the marinade from the ham into the mixture. With the wooden spoon, beat the mixture until it draws from the side of the bowl, 1–2 minutes.

9 Wipe the frying pan with paper towels. Add a little of the meat mixture and fry until browned on both sides, 1–2 minutes. Taste, and add more spices and salt and pepper if needed.

ANNE SAYS
"The mixture should be quite spicy."

2 ASSEMBLE AND BAKE THE TERRINE

2 Spoon half of the meat mixture into the terrine, then arrange the ham strips lengthways, end to end, on the top.

Piece of barding fat is reserved to top meat mixture

1 Heat the oven to 180°C (350°F, Gas 4). Set aside 1 piece of barding fat and use the rest to line the bottom and longer sides of the terrine mould.

3 Spread the remaining meat mixture over the ham, fold over the barding fat overhanging the sides of the terrine, then top with the reserved barding fat and the bay leaf. Cover the terrine with the lid.

Meat mixture is spread evenly over ham strips

Overhanging barding fat will be folded over top of terrine before baking

4 Put the flour and water into a small bowl and mix together to make a soft smooth paste.

5 Using your fingers, seal the gap between the rim of the mould and the lid with the paste.

7 Bake the terrine until the metal skewer inserted into the terrine for 30 seconds is hot to the touch when withdrawn, 1¼–1½ hours. Remove the terrine from the water bath and let it cool to tepid.

8 Remove the lid, cover the terrine, and set a weight on top. Chill for at least 1 day to allow the flavours to mellow.

ANNE SAYS
"A 500 g (1 lb) weight is just heavy enough to compress the terrine so it slices well."

6 Set the mould in the roasting tin. Add boiling water to come halfway up the sides. Bring this water bath to a boil on top of the stove, then transfer the terrine in the tin to the oven.

Small knife loosens lid easily

3 FINISH THE TERRINE

Fan shapes are pretty alternative to whole gherkins

Press lightly on gherkin fans to flatten them

1 Cut each gherkin lengthways into 4–5 slices, leaving them attached at the stalk ends.

2 Using your thumb or finger and thumb, flatten each gherkin to make it into a fan shape.

3 With a metal spoon, scrape away and discard any fat from the top of the terrine.

Hardened fat is easy to remove

4 Dip a small knife into hot water and run it around the sides of the terrine to make it easier to turn out.

6 Using the chef's knife, cut the terrine into slices about 1 cm (3/8 inch) thick.

Slice carefully so terrine doesn't crumble

5 Holding the terrine mould with both hands, turn out the terrine onto a chopping board.

7 Arrange the terrine slices on individual plates or a large platter and decorate with the gherkin fans.

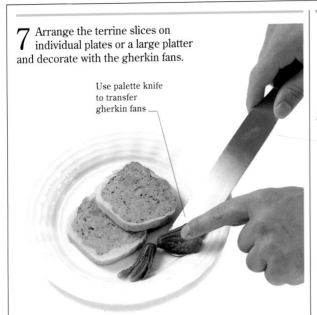

Use palette knife to transfer gherkin fans

🍽 **TO SERVE**
Serve the terrine with pickled onions and crusty bread.

Barding fat is discarded before eating

Terrine can be served slightly chilled or at room temperature

GAME TERRINE
TERRINE DE GIBIER

Venison replaces the minced veal in this terrine, popular in the autumn when hunting is a favourite French pastime. If venison is not available, you can replace it with the same weight of minced pheasant or rabbit.

1 Omit the ham, minced veal, and gherkins. Cut a 125 g (4 oz) piece of venison into strips 1 cm (3/8 inch) wide. With the flat side of a chef's knife, crush 3 juniper berries. Combine the juniper berries, brandy, and salt and pepper in a bowl. Add the venison strips and marinate as directed for the ham.

2 Make the meat mixture as directed, using 250 g (8 oz) minced venison in place of the veal and adding 60 g (2 oz) shelled pistachio nuts with the minced meat. Cook a small portion of the meat mixture, then taste for seasoning.

3 Assemble the terrine, lining the mould with 250 g (8 oz) bacon rashers instead of the barding fat and replacing the ham with the venison strips. Bake and unmould the terrine and slice as directed.

QUICHE LORRAINE

🍽 SERVES 6 🥣 WORK TIME 45–50 MINUTES* BAKING TIME 30–35 MINUTES

EQUIPMENT

chef's knife

whisk

25 cm (10 inch) flan tin with removable base

ladle

rolling pin

slotted spoon

pastry brush

medium frying pan

scissors

bowls

paper towels

wire rack

sieve

baking sheet

grater

cling film

pastry scraper

aluminium foil

dried beans or rice

INGREDIENTS

thick-cut bacon rashers

Gruyère cheese

egg yolks

plain flour

ground nutmeg

single cream

eggs

unsalted butter

ANNE SAYS
"For a lighter filling, replace half of the cream with milk."

Quiche, now known in many variations throughout the world, comes from the Lorraine in eastern France. Purists say it should be flavoured only with bacon, but I like to add some grated Gruyère cheese. Serve it warm or at room temperature but never very hot as the custard will be too soft.

GETTING AHEAD
The pâte brisée dough can be made up to 2 days ahead and kept, tightly wrapped, in the refrigerator. The quiche is best on the day of baking.

*plus 45 minutes chilling time

metric	SHOPPING LIST	imperial
250 g	thick-cut bacon rashers	8 oz
75 g	Gruyère cheese	2¹/₂ oz
	For the pâte brisée dough	
175 g	plain flour, more for work surface	6 oz
1	egg yolk	1
2.5 ml	salt	¹/₂ tsp
45 ml	water, more if needed	3 tbsp
90 g	unsalted butter, more for flan tin	3 oz
	For the custard	
500 ml	single cream	16 fl oz
1	pinch of ground nutmeg	1
	salt and pepper	
1	egg yolk	1
3	eggs	3

ORDER OF WORK

1 MAKE THE PATE BRISEE DOUGH

2 LINE THE FLAN TIN

3 BAKE THE PASTRY SHELL BLIND

4 MAKE THE FILLING AND BAKE THE QUICHE

1 MAKE THE PATE BRISEE DOUGH

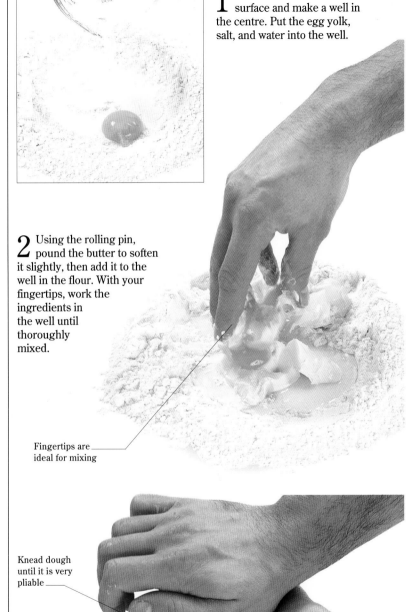

1 Sift the flour onto the work surface and make a well in the centre. Put the egg yolk, salt, and water into the well.

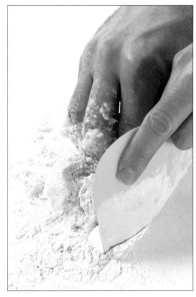

2 Using the rolling pin, pound the butter to soften it slightly, then add it to the well in the flour. With your fingertips, work the ingredients in the well until thoroughly mixed.

Fingertips are ideal for mixing

3 Draw in the flour with the pastry scraper. With your fingers, work the flour into the other ingredients until coarse crumbs form. Press the dough into a ball.

ANNE SAYS
"If the crumbs are dry, sprinkle them with a little more water before pressing the dough together."

Knead dough until it is very pliable

4 Lightly flour the work surface, then blend the dough by pushing it away from you with the heel of your hand. Gather it up with the pastry scraper and continue to blend until it is very smooth and peels away from the work surface in one piece, 1–2 minutes.

5 Shape the dough into a ball, wrap it tightly in cling film, and chill until firm, about 30 minutes.

2 LINE THE FLAN TIN

Dough is easy to lift when wrapped around rolling pin

1 Brush the flan tin with melted butter. Lightly flour the work surface. Roll out the chilled dough into a 30 cm (12 inch) round. Wrap the dough around the rolling pin and unroll it so that it drapes over the tin and hangs over the edge.

! TAKE CARE !
Be careful not to stretch the dough or it will shrink when baked.

2 Gently lift the edge of the dough with one hand and press it well into the bottom edge of the tin with the forefinger of the other hand.

3 Roll the rolling pin over the top of the tin, pressing down to cut off the excess dough.

4 With your forefingers and thumb, press the dough evenly up the side, from the bottom, to increase the height of the dough shell.

5 Prick the bottom of the shell lightly with a fork to prevent air bubbles from forming during baking. Chill until firm, at least 15 minutes.

3 BAKE THE PASTRY SHELL BLIND

Dried chick peas are good for baking blind

Double thickness of foil helps dough keep its shape during baking

1 Heat the oven to 200°C (400°F, Gas 6). Put the baking sheet into the oven to heat. Line the pastry shell with a double thickness of foil, pressing it well into the bottom edge. Trim the foil if necessary, using the scissors, so that it stands about 4 cm (1 1/2 inches) above the edge of the tin.

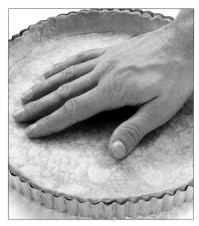

2 Spread a layer of dried beans or rice over the foil to weigh down the dough while it is baking.

3 Place the flan tin on the baking sheet and bake the pastry shell in the heated oven until set and the rim starts to brown, about 10 minutes. Carefully remove the foil and beans or rice.

4 Reduce the oven temperature to 190°C (375°F, Gas 5). Continue baking until the pastry is lightly browned, 5–8 minutes longer. Remove the pastry shell from the oven and let cool slightly. Leave the oven on.

4 MAKE THE FILLING AND BAKE THE QUICHE

1 Stack the bacon rashers on a chopping board and cut them crossways into 5 mm (1/4 inch) strips.

2 Put the bacon into the frying pan, and cook, stirring occasionally, until lightly browned, 3–4 minutes.

Paper towels absorb excess fat from bacon

Bacon should be soft, not crispy

3 Using the slotted spoon, lift the bacon out of the frying pan and transfer to paper towels to drain.

4 Put the cream, nutmeg, and salt and pepper into a bowl. Add the egg yolk and eggs and whisk until thoroughly mixed.

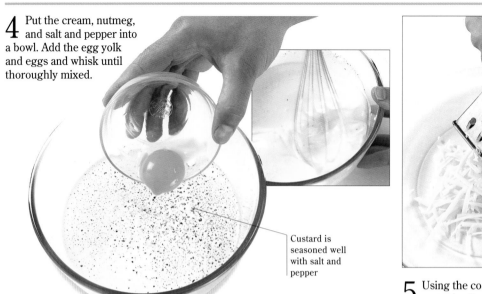

Custard is seasoned well with salt and pepper

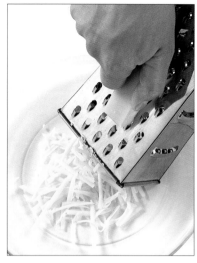

5 Using the coarse side of the grater, grate the Gruyère cheese onto a plate and set aside.

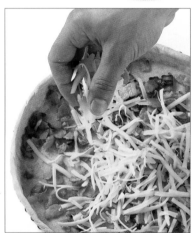

6 Sprinkle the bacon pieces and grated cheese evenly over the bottom of the pastry shell.

7 Set the flan tin on the baking sheet. Whisk the custard mixture and ladle it over the bacon and cheese. Bake the quiche in the heated oven until lightly browned and the custard is set, 30–35 minutes.

ANNE SAYS
"*If the top is not brown, heat the grill and grill the quiche if you like, 1–2 minutes. If the custard gets too brown during baking, cover the quiche loosely with a piece of foil.*"

Heated baking sheet ensures quiche bakes crisply

Bacon and cheese are covered with even layer of custard

VARIATION

LEEK AND CHEESE QUICHE

QUICHE AUX POIREAUX ET FROMAGE

Leeks are the only green vegetable found in our garden during the long Burgundian winter. I like to cook them until tender, then bake them in this quiche flavoured with cheese.

8 Let the quiche cool slightly on the wire rack, then set the flan tin on a bowl to loosen and remove the side. Transfer the quiche to a chopping board or serving platter.

🍽 TO SERVE

Serve the quiche cut into wedges, warm or at room temperature. Accompany with a salad, if you like.

1 Omit the bacon rashers. Make the pâte brisée dough, line the flan tin, and bake the pastry shell blind as directed. Leave the oven on.

Gruyère-flavoured custard is soft and golden

2 Trim 4 medium leeks (total weight about 375 g/12 oz), discarding the roots and tough green tops. With a chef's knife, slit the leeks lengthways in half and wash them thoroughly under cold running water. Place each half, cut-side down, on a chopping board. Fan the leek slightly so that it lies flat, then cut each leek crossways into 1.25 cm (1/2 inch) slices.

3 Heat 30 g (1 oz) butter in a frying pan. Add the leeks and season with salt and pepper. Press a piece of buttered foil on top of the leeks and cover with a lid. Cook the leeks over very low heat, stirring occasionally, until they are very soft, 20–25 minutes. Do not allow the leeks to brown.

4 Heat the baking sheet as directed. Make the custard and grate 90 g (3 oz) Gruyère cheese as directed. With a slotted spoon, transfer the sliced leeks to the pastry shell. Set the flan tin on the heated baking sheet, whisk the custard, and ladle it over the leeks. Sprinkle with the grated cheese and bake the quiche as directed.

Seasonal salad is the classic partner for a slice of Quiche Lorraine

BUCKWHEAT CREPES WITH SEAFOOD

Galettes de Sarrasin aux Fruits de Mer

 SERVES 6   WORK TIME 45–50 MINUTES   BAKING TIME 15–20 MINUTES

EQUIPMENT

chef's knife

palette knife

small ladle

20 cm (8 inch) crêpe pan

whisk

paper towels

slotted spoon

small knife

pastry brush

baking dish

sieve

wooden spoon

bowls

colander

saucepans, 1 with lid, 1 heavy-based

chopping board

Brittany is renowned for its seafood, but the soil is too thin to grow much wheat. Buckwheat is more adaptable, hence the traditional Breton buckwheat crêpes, filled here with a creamy seafood mixture.

INGREDIENTS

skinned sole fillets

scallops

milk

cooked peeled prawns

mushrooms

ground nutmeg

double cream

fresh tarragon

butter

fish stock

plain flour

eggs

lemon juice

buckwheat flour

metric	SHOPPING LIST	imperial
375 g	skinned sole fillets	12 oz
175 g	scallops	6 oz
175 g	cooked peeled prawns	6 oz
125 g	mushrooms	4 oz
5–7	sprigs of fresh tarragon	5–7
750 ml	fish stock (see box, page 123)	1¼ pints
	juice of ½ lemon	
125 ml	water	4 fl oz
90 g	butter	3 oz
75 g	plain flour	2½ oz
1	pinch of ground nutmeg	1
150 ml	double cream	5 fl oz
	salt and pepper	
	For the crêpe batter	
60 g	butter, more if needed	2 oz
100 g	buckwheat flour	3½ oz
30 g	plain flour	1 oz
2.5 ml	salt	½ tsp
3	eggs	3
300 ml	milk	½ pint

ORDER OF WORK

1 MAKE THE CREPE BATTER

2 PREPARE THE FILLING

3 COOK THE FILLING AND MAKE THE SAUCE

4 FRY THE CREPES AND FINISH THE DISH

1 MAKE THE CREPE BATTER

1 Melt the butter in a small saucepan and set aside to cool. Sift both of the flours and the salt into a bowl.

2 Make a well in the centre of the flour, add the eggs, and whisk until they are thoroughly mixed.

3 Pour half of the milk into the mixture in a slow, steady stream, whisking constantly and gradually drawing in the flour to make a smooth batter. Stir in half of the melted butter and half of the remaining milk. Cover the batter and let stand, 30 minutes. Meanwhile, prepare the filling.

Milk is added gradually so that no lumps form in batter

2 PREPARE THE FILLING

1 Using the chef's knife, cut the sole fillets into 2 cm (¾ inch) strips. Season the fish with salt and pepper.

2 If necessary, discard the tough, crescent-shaped membrane at the side of each scallop. Rinse the scallops with cold water, drain, then cut them into quarters.

Fresh scallops are creamy white

Scallops are cut into bite-sized pieces

3 Reserve 6 prawns for decoration. Cut the remaining prawns lengthways and then crossways in half. Put the quartered prawns into a bowl.

4 Wipe the mushroom caps with damp paper towels and trim the stalks even with the caps. Set the caps stalk-side down and cut into quarters.

5 Strip the tarragon leaves from the stalks and pile the leaves on the chopping board. Coarsely chop them with the chef's knife.

3 COOK THE FILLING AND MAKE THE SAUCE

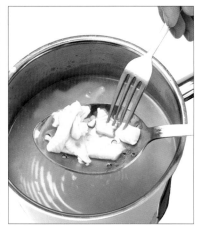

1 In a medium saucepan, bring the fish stock to a boil. Add the sole strips and simmer until they just flake easily with a fork, 1–2 minutes.

Once cooked, fish becomes opaque

Sole breaks into smaller pieces after cooking

2 Lift out the sole strips with the slotted spoon and add them to the bowl with the prawns.

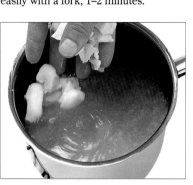

3 Add the scallops to the fish stock. Simmer just until tender, 1–2 minutes. Transfer the scallops to the bowl of fish. Reserve the stock.

4 Put the mushrooms, lemon juice, water, and salt and pepper in a medium saucepan. Cover, and cook over high heat until the liquid boils to the top of the pan and the mushrooms are tender, 3–5 minutes.

5 With the slotted spoon, transfer the mushrooms to the bowl of seafood. Add their cooking liquid to the fish stock.

Mushroom cooking liquid is full of flavour

6 Make the sauce: melt the butter in the heavy-based saucepan over medium heat. Whisk in the flour and cook until foaming, 30–60 seconds.

7 Take the saucepan from the heat, let cool slightly, then strain in the fish stock and whisk to mix.

Sauce binds seafood and mushrooms

8 Return the saucepan to the heat and cook, whisking constantly, until the sauce boils and thickens. Season with the nutmeg, and salt and pepper to taste. Simmer the sauce until it is well flavoured and thickly coats the back of a spoon, about 5 minutes.

9 Add half of the sauce to the seafood mixture. Reserve 15 ml (1 tbsp) of the tarragon for decoration, add the rest to the mixture, and stir until combined. Taste for seasoning. Set the remaining sauce aside while frying the crêpes.

4 FRY THE CREPES AND FINISH THE DISH

1 Using the wooden spoon, stir enough of the remaining milk into the batter to make it the consistency of thin cream. Brush the baking dish with melted butter.

2 Add the remaining melted butter to the crêpe pan and heat gently. Pour the excess into a bowl, leaving a thin film. Add a little batter and wait to see if it splutters, showing the pan is hot.

3 Using the small ladle, add some batter to the pan, rotating and shaking the pan at the same time so that the batter coats the base evenly and completely.

Lift crêpe with palette knife

4 Fry the crêpe quickly over medium heat until it is set on top and brown underneath, 1–2 minutes. Loosen it with the palette knife and toss or turn it. Continue cooking until brown on the other side, 30–60 seconds. Transfer the crêpe to a plate.

5 Continue with the remaining batter, adding more melted butter to the pan as necessary, to make a total of 12 crêpes. Pile the crêpes on the plate so that they stay moist and warm.

Crêpes are stacked in neat pile

Roll up crêpe starting with unfolded side

6 Heat the oven to 180°C (350°F, Gas 4). Put 30 ml (2 tbsp) of filling into the centre of each crêpe, fold in 2 sides, and roll into a cylinder. Arrange seam-side down in the baking dish.

7 Add the cream to the remaining sauce and bring to a boil, stirring constantly. Taste for seasoning.

8 Pour the sauce over the crêpes so they are completely coated. Bake the crêpes in the heated oven until the filling is hot and the sauce is bubbling, 15–20 minutes.

Sauce coats crêpes so they stay moist during baking

Prawn garnish echoes seafood filling

 TO SERVE

Arrange the 6 reserved prawns in the middle of the dish, and sprinkle with the reserved tarragon. Serve at once, directly from the baking dish, allowing 2 crêpes per person.

Sauce turns golden brown during baking

BUCKWHEAT CREPES WITH HAM

GALETTES DE SARRASIN AU JAMBON

Ham and cheese replace the seafood filling in this version of buckwheat crêpes.

1 Omit the seafood filling and sauce. Brush 6 individual gratin dishes with butter. Make the buckwheat crêpes as directed. Replace the seafood mixture with 250 g (8 oz) thinly sliced cooked ham. Coarsely grate 250 g (8 oz) Gruyère cheese. Reserve 30 g (1 oz) of the grated cheese for topping.

2 Arrange a slice of cooked ham on a crêpe, then sprinkle it with 15–30 ml (1–2 tbsp) of the grated cheese. Fold the crêpe in half, then in half again to form a triangle. Repeat for the remaining crêpes.

3 Put 2 crêpes into each gratin dish and bake in the heated oven until hot, 10–15 minutes. Sprinkle the remaining cheese on top of each serving and bake the crêpes just until the cheese is melted, 3–5 minutes.

GETTING AHEAD

The crêpes can be made up to 2 days ahead, layered with greaseproof paper, and kept, tightly wrapped, in the refrigerator. The dish can be assembled up to 12 hours ahead and kept in the refrigerator, or it can be frozen. Bake it just before serving.

OMELETTE WITH PEPPERS AND TOMATOES

Omelette Basquaise

 SERVES 2   WORK TIME 20–25 MINUTES   COOKING TIME 15–25 MINUTES

EQUIPMENT

bowls

23 cm (9 inch) omelette pan

medium frying pan

medium saucepan

 wooden spoon

 slotted spoon

 rubber gloves

chef's knife

small knife

 chopping board

In the Basque country at the western end of the Pyrenees, hot and sweet peppers of all kinds are a staple. Most varieties are local to the region, so here I suggest a mixture of peppers spiced with a chilli or two. The omelette itself is browned on both sides, like a Spanish tortilla.

GETTING AHEAD

The Basquaise filling can be prepared 1 day ahead and kept, covered, in the refrigerator. The omelette should not be cooked until just before serving.

metric	SHOPPING LIST	imperial
1	medium onion	1
2	garlic cloves	2
1	red pepper	1
1–2	small hot red chillies	1–2
250 g	tomatoes	8 oz
1	small bunch of parsley	1
60 g	butter	2 oz
5	eggs	5
	salt and pepper	

INGREDIENTS

 eggs

 parsley

 red pepper

 small hot red chillies

 butter

 tomatoes

garlic cloves

 onion

ORDER OF WORK

1 PREPARE THE BASQUAISE FILLING

2 COOK THE OMELETTE

1 PREPARE THE BASQUAISE FILLING

1 Peel the onion, leaving a little of the root attached, then cut it lengthways in half. Lay each onion half flat and cut it across into thin slices.

2 Set the flat side of the chef's knife on top of each garlic clove and strike it with your fist.

3 Peel the skin from the garlic cloves with your fingers. Finely chop the cloves with the chef's knife.

Seeds and ribs are easily cut away

4 With the small knife, cut around the red pepper core. Twist the core with your fingers, pull it out, and discard it.

5 Halve the pepper lengthways and scrape out the seeds. Cut away the white ribs on the inside. Set each pepper half, cut-side down, on the chopping board, flatten it with the heel of your hand, and slice it lengthways into thin strips.

6 Cut each chilli lengthways in half with the small knife. Cut out and discard the core. Scrape out the seeds and cut away the white ribs from each half.

! TAKE CARE !
Wear rubber gloves when preparing fresh chillies, as they can burn your skin.

Rubber gloves protect hands

7 Cut each chilli half into very thin strips, gather the strips together, and cut across into fine dice.

After tomatoes are blanched, skins slip off easily

8 Cut the cores from the tomatoes and score an "x" on the base of each one. Immerse the tomatoes in boiling water until the skins start to split, 8–15 seconds. Transfer them at once to cold water with a slotted spoon. When cool, peel, then halve the tomatoes crossways. Squeeze out the seeds and coarsely chop each tomato half.

9 Strip the parsley leaves from the stalks and pile the leaves on the chopping board. With the chef's knife, finely chop them.

11 Add the chopped tomatoes, garlic, and salt and pepper, and continue cooking until the mixture is thick and most of the liquid has evaporated, 5–10 minutes longer. Remove from the heat, stir in the chopped parsley, and taste the filling for seasoning.

Parsley is added after vegetables are cooked

10 Melt half of the butter in the frying pan, add the onion, red pepper, and chillies, and cook, stirring occasionally, until the vegetables just begin to soften, 5–8 minutes.

2 COOK THE OMELETTE

2 Quickly but carefully pull the cooked egg mixture from the side of the pan to the centre, then tip the pan so the uncooked egg mixture flows to the side. Continue this until the eggs are partly set, about 30 seconds.

1 Crack the eggs into a bowl, add salt and pepper, and beat with a fork until thoroughly mixed. Melt the remaining butter in the omelette pan over high heat. When it stops foaming and starts to brown, pour in the eggs. Stir briskly with the flat of the fork until the eggs start to thicken, 8–10 seconds.

Edge of omelette is lifted so uncooked egg runs underneath

Heavy pan is best for good omelette

3 Stir the Basquaise filling into the egg mixture and continue stirring until well mixed, 3–5 seconds. Lower the heat and leave the omelette to cook undisturbed until it is set on top and browned underneath, 2–3 minutes longer.

ANNE SAYS
"Cooking the omelette without stirring allows the bottom to brown evenly."

4 Remove the pan from the heat. Place a large plate over the top of the omelette pan and invert both the pan and plate to turn out the omelette. Slide it back into the pan and brown the other side, 30–60 seconds.

Omelette is flipped to brown both sides

🍽 TO SERVE
Slide the omelette onto a warmed serving plate. Cut it into wedges and serve hot or at room temperature.

Crisp salad is colourful accompaniment to omelette

Golden omelette is filled with sweet onions and peppers

VARIATION
COUNTRY OMELETTE
OMELETTE PAYSANNE
This omelette, filled with potatoes, onion, and bacon, is typical fare in French cafés.

1 Omit the garlic, red pepper, chillies, and tomatoes. Slice the onion and chop the parsley as directed, reserving 1–2 small parsley sprigs for decoration.
2 Stack 250 g (8 oz) streaky bacon rashers on a chopping board and cut them crossways into strips. Peel 500 g (1 lb) potatoes and square off the sides. Cut the potatoes into 1 cm (3/8 inch) slices, stack the slices, and cut them into 1 cm (3/8 inch) strips. Gather the strips together into a pile and cut crossways into cubes.
3 Heat the bacon in a large frying pan and cook over medium heat, stirring occasionally, until the fat is rendered (melted), 3–5 minutes. Discard all but 30 ml (2 tbsp) of the bacon fat. Stir in the onion and potatoes and continue cooking, stirring occasionally, until the onion and potatoes are tender and golden, 15–20 minutes longer. Season to taste with salt and pepper. Cook the omelette as directed, adding the potato mixture in place of the Basquaise filling.
4 To serve, cut the omelette into wedges and decorate with the reserved parsley sprigs.

SCALLOPS WITH TOMATOES, GARLIC, AND HERBS

Coquilles St Jacques à la Provençale

 SERVES 4–6   WORK TIME 15–20 MINUTES   COOKING TIME 15–20 MINUTES

EQUIPMENT

wooden spoon

chef's knife

small knife

large frying pan

slotted spoon

bowls

medium saucepan

medium sauté pan

chopping board

paper towels

INGREDIENTS

scallops

fresh basil

garlic cloves

tomatoes

fresh thyme

dry white wine

olive oil

butter

Opinions vary on what constitutes an authentic Provençal garnish for scallops. Olive oil and chopped garlic are clearly mandatory but debate can become heated on the value of tomatoes, chopped and added as a concassée. *Personally, I always like to include them.*

GETTING AHEAD

The tomatoes can be prepared up to 1 day ahead and kept, covered, in the refrigerator. Sauté the scallops and finish the dish just before serving.

metric	SHOPPING LIST	imperial
750 g	tomatoes	1 1/2 lb
3	garlic cloves	3
5–7	sprigs of fresh basil	5–7
7–10	sprigs of fresh thyme	7–10
30 ml	olive oil	2 tbsp
175 ml	dry white wine	6 fl oz
	salt and pepper	
750 g	large or Queen scallops	1 1/2 lb
30 g	butter	1 oz
	rice pilaf (see box, page 42) for serving (optional)	

ORDER OF WORK

1 PREPARE THE TOMATO MIXTURE

2 COOK THE SCALLOPS AND FINISH THE DISH

1 PREPARE THE TOMATO MIXTURE

Seeds are removed before tomatoes are chopped

2 Lightly crush each garlic clove with the flat of the chef's knife. Discard the skin and finely chop the cloves.

1 Core the tomatoes and score an "x" on the base of each. Immerse in boiling water until the skins start to split, 8–15 seconds. Transfer at once to cold water. When cool, peel, then halve crossways. Squeeze out the seeds, then coarsely chop each tomato half.

3 Strip the basil leaves from the stalks and finely chop the leaves. Strip the thyme leaves from the stalks.

Tomatoes and wine cook into thick sauce

Basil and thyme flavour tomatoes

4 Heat 15 ml (1 tbsp) of the oil in the sauté pan. Add the chopped garlic and cook over medium heat, stirring occasionally, until soft, 2–3 minutes.

5 Stir in the tomatoes, basil, thyme, wine, and salt and pepper. Simmer over medium heat, stirring occasionally, until thick enough to just fall easily from the spoon, 10–15 minutes. Taste for seasoning.

2 COOK THE SCALLOPS AND FINISH THE DISH

1 If necessary, discard the tough, crescent-shaped membrane at the side of each scallop.

2 Rinse the scallops with cold water, pat dry with paper towels, and season them with salt and pepper.

RICE PILAF

When making pilaf, the rice is first quickly fried in vegetable oil to help keep the grains separate as the rice simmers. It is then cooked in a measured amount of water so the liquid is all absorbed during cooking, leaving the rice light, tender, and flaky.

🍽 SERVES 4–6

🥣 WORK TIME 9–10 MINUTES

🍲 COOKING TIME 20 MINUTES*

* plus 10 minutes standing time

SHOPPING LIST

1	medium onion	1
30 ml	vegetable oil	2 tbsp
300 g	long-grain rice	10 oz
750 ml	water	1¹/₄ pints
	salt and pepper	

1 Peel and chop the onion into dice. Heat the oil in a heavy-based saucepan, add the onion, and cook, stirring, until soft, 3–5 minutes.

2 Add the rice and cook, stirring, until the oil is absorbed and the rice looks translucent, 2–3 minutes.

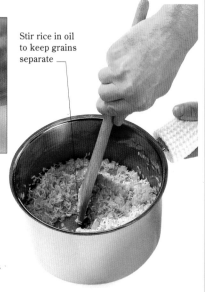

Stir rice in oil to keep grains separate

3 Pour the water into the saucepan, season the rice with salt and pepper, and bring to a boil.

4 Cover the pan, reduce the heat, and simmer until all the liquid is absorbed and the rice is tender, about 20 minutes. Let stand, still covered, 10 minutes, then stir with a fork.

3 Heat the butter and the remaining oil in the large frying pan. Cook the scallops until brown and slightly crisp on one side, 1 minute for Queen scallops, 2 minutes for large scallops.

4 Turn the scallops, stir in the tomato mixture, and continue cooking, 1–2 minutes.

ANNE SAYS
"The scallops should cook over high heat so the outsides become crisp, while the centres remain tender. Do not overcook them or they will be tough."

🍴 TO SERVE
Serve the scallops at once on a warmed platter. Accompany with rice pilaf, if you like.

Lemon wedges are served alongside scallops

Rich Provençal sauce coats tender scallops

V A R I A T I O N

SPICED SCALLOPS
COQUILLES ST JACQUES NANTAISE
This spicy dish comes from Nantes, in southern Brittany.

1 Omit the garlic, basil, and thyme. Brush 4 individual heatproof dishes with melted butter. Finely chop 250 g (8 oz) tomatoes as directed. Peel a small onion and cut it lengthways in half. Lay each half flat and slice horizontally, then vertically towards the root, leaving the slices attached. Finally, cut across into fine dice. Trim the crusts from 2 slices of white bread. Work the slices in a food processor to form crumbs.
2 Heat 15 ml (1 tbsp) olive oil and 15 g (1/2 oz) butter in a large frying pan with 1.25 ml (1/4 tsp) curry powder and a pinch of cayenne. Cook 500 g (1 lb) scallops until brown and slightly crisp, 1 minute for Queen scallops, 2 minutes for large scallops. Turn and continue cooking, 1–2 minutes. Put the scallops into the prepared heatproof dishes and cover with foil.
3 Heat the grill. Melt 15 g (1/2 oz) butter in the frying pan, then add the onion. Cook, stirring occasionally, until soft, 3–5 minutes. Add 30 ml (2 tbsp) brandy with the white wine and bring to a boil. Stir in the tomatoes and salt and pepper, and cook until the tomatoes are pulpy, 6–8 minutes. Taste for seasoning, then spoon the mixture over the scallops. Stir 15 g (1/2 oz) melted butter into the breadcrumbs and sprinkle over the tomato mixture. Grill until the breadcrumbs are browned, 2–3 minutes. Serves 4.

ROAST SEA BASS WITH HERB BUTTER SAUCE

Loup Rôti au Beurre de Montpellier

 SERVES 4   WORK TIME 40–45 MINUTES   ROASTING TIME 30–40 MINUTES

EQUIPMENT

large roasting tin

colander

lemon squeezer

food processor†

paper towels

medium saucepan

kitchen scissors

rubber spatula

palette knife

chef's knife

small knife

chopping board

†blender can also be used

A whole sea bass is roasted with thyme and lemon, then served with a herb butter sauce.

GETTING AHEAD
The herb butter sauce can be prepared up to 1 day ahead, and the flavours will mellow. Keep it, covered, in the refrigerator and let it come to room temperature before serving. The fish is best roasted just before serving.

metric	SHOPPING LIST	imperial
1	whole sea bass, weighing about 2 kg (4 1/2 lb), cleaned and scaled	1
3–5	sprigs of fresh thyme	3–5
30 g	butter	1 oz
125 ml	dry white wine	4 fl oz
	salt and pepper	
For the herb butter sauce		
8	spinach leaves, total weight 15 g (1/2 oz)	8
1	bunch of watercress, weighing about 30 g (1 oz)	1
10–12	sprigs of parsley, total weight 15 g (1/2 oz)	10–12
10–12	sprigs of fresh chervil, total weight 15 g (1/2 oz)	10–12
1	garlic clove	1
1	lemon	1
2	anchovy fillets	2
10 ml	capers, drained	2 tsp
1	small gherkin	1
75 g	butter	2 1/2 oz
45 ml	olive oil	3 tbsp
5 ml	Dijon mustard	1 tsp

INGREDIENTS

sea bass

watercress

capers

fresh chervil

parsley

olive oil

spinach

butter

small gherkin

fresh thyme

garlic clove

dry white wine

lemon

anchovy fillets

Dijon mustard

ANNE SAYS
"If sea bass is not available, you can substitute salmon trout or sea bream."

ORDER OF WORK

1 MAKE THE HERB BUTTER SAUCE

2 ROAST THE SEA BASS

1 MAKE THE HERB BUTTER SAUCE

Fresh young leaves are used for sauce

1 Discard any tough ribs and stalks from the spinach and watercress and wash the leaves in plenty of cold water. Set aside half of the watercress for garnish.

2 Strip the parsley and chervil leaves from the stalks, and add them to the spinach and watercress. Drain thoroughly.

3 Bring a medium saucepan of salted water to a boil. Add the spinach, watercress, parsley, and chervil, and simmer until tender, 1–2 minutes. Drain in the colander.

4 Rinse the greens with cold water and drain again thoroughly. Squeeze in your fist to remove excess water.

ANNE SAYS
"Rinsing the greens in cold water helps them keep their bright green colour."

5 Set the flat side of the chef's knife on top of the garlic clove and strike it with your fist. Discard the skin.

6 Cut the lemon lengthways in half. Set one half, flat-side down, on the chopping board, cut it crossways into thin slices, and reserve for cooking the fish. Squeeze the juice from the remaining lemon half.

Lemon juice flavours sauce

8 With the blade turning, slowly pour in the olive oil. Add the lemon juice, mustard, and salt and pepper, and work again briefly. Taste for seasoning, remove, and set aside.

Mustard is added after greens have been chopped

7 In the food processor, work the garlic, anchovy fillets, capers, and gherkin until finely chopped. Add the butter, piece by piece, and work the mixture to a smooth purée. Add the greens and work until finely chopped.

2 ROAST THE SEA BASS

Scissors are good for trimming fish

Fins are snipped off for attractive presentation

1 Heat the oven to 190°C (375°F, Gas 5). Cut the fins from the sea bass with the scissors. Trim the tail to a V-shape.

2 Rinse the fish thoroughly inside and out with cold water and pat dry with paper towels.

3 With the chef's knife, slash the fish diagonally 3–4 times on each side. The slashes should be about 1.25 cm (1/2 inch) deep for heat to penetrate.

4 Set the sea bass in the roasting tin and tuck a sprig of thyme and a slice of lemon into each slash.

5 Dot the fish with the butter and sprinkle with white wine, and salt and pepper.

Wine and butter flavour roasted sea bass

VARIATION

LOIRE SEA BASS

LOUP ROTI, SAUCE BEURRE BLANC

Beurre blanc originated in Brittany, near the River Loire.

6 Roast the fish, basting occasionally, until it just flakes easily when tested with a fork, 30–40 minutes.

ANNE SAYS
"The fish is done when the flesh is no longer transparent in the centre."

1 Omit the herb butter sauce. Roast 2 cleaned and scaled sea bass (each weighing about 1 kg/2 lb) as directed, replacing the thyme sprigs with fresh tarragon, 25–30 minutes.

2 While the fish are roasting, make the sauce: peel 2 shallots and cut them in half. Slice horizontally, then vertically, leaving the slices attached. Cut across to make dice.

3 In a small heavy-based pan, combine 45 ml (3 tbsp) each white wine vinegar and dry white wine with the shallots, then boil until reduced to about 15 ml (1 tbsp), 3–5 minutes. Add 15 ml (1 tbsp) double cream, bring to a boil, and reduce to 15 ml (1 tbsp). Cut 250 g (8 oz) cold butter into small pieces. Whisk the butter into the shallots, moving the pan on and off the heat so that the butter emulsifies, thickening the sauce lightly. Do not let the base of the pan get more than hand-hot. Taste the sauce for seasoning. Keep it warm on a rack over a pan of warm water until serving.

4 Cut each fish in half and remove the head and tail. Serve with the sauce.

🍽️ **TO SERVE**

Transfer the fish to a warmed platter and decorate with the reserved watercress. Serve hot or at room temperature, with the herb butter sauce handed separately.

Lemon and thyme decoration echoes flavouring of roast sea bass

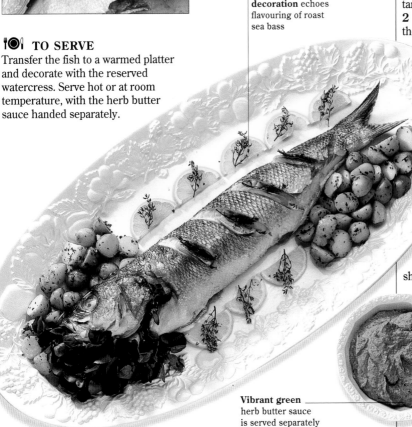

Vibrant green herb butter sauce is served separately

SWEET-SOUR DUCK WITH CHERRIES

Canard aux Cerises à l'Aigre-doux

EQUIPMENT

slotted spoon

wooden spoon

sieve

2-pronged fork

small knife

bowls

metal spoon

roasting tin

cherry stoner†

saucepans,
1 small heavy-based

trussing needle
and kitchen string

aluminium foil

paper towels

†vegetable peeler can also be used

Tart cherries are the key to this preparation of crisply roasted duck from the Limousin in the centre of France, where cherries grow wild in the hedgerows. A mixture of caramel and red wine vinegar, added to the pan at the end of cooking, lends the sweet-sour flavour to the sauce.

INGREDIENTS

duck

tart cherries

sugar

watercress

beef or
veal stock

vegetable
oil

red wine
vinegar

ANNE SAYS
"If fresh tart cherries are not available, you can use a 500 g (1 lb) can of tart cherries packed in water."

ORDER OF WORK

1 TRUSS THE DUCK

2 ROAST THE DUCK

3 PREPARE THE CARAMEL VINEGAR AND THE CHERRIES

4 FINISH THE SAUCE AND CARVE THE DUCK

metric	SHOPPING LIST	imperial
1	duck, weighing about 1.8 kg (4 lb)	1
15 ml	vegetable oil	1 tbsp
75 ml	water	2½ fl oz
60 g	granulated sugar	2 oz
75 ml	red wine vinegar	2½ fl oz
375 g	tart cherries	12 oz
375 ml	beef or veal stock (see box, page 123)	12 fl oz
	salt and pepper	
1	small bunch of watercress for decoration (optional)	1

1 TRUSS THE DUCK

1 Wipe the inside of the duck with paper towels and season it inside and out with salt and pepper. Pull any loose bits of fat from the skin and discard them.

2 With the small knife, remove the wishbone to make the duck easier to carve.

Hold legs of duck firmly in place while pushing through trussing needle

3 Set the duck breast-side up. Push the legs back and down. Push the trussing needle into the flesh at the knee joint, through the bird and out through the other knee joint.

4 Turn the duck over. Pull the neck skin over the neck cavity and tuck the wing tips over it. Push the needle through one of the wings into the neck skin. Continue under the backbone of the duck to the other side. Repeat with the second wing.

Trussing string keeps duck in shape so it cooks evenly

5 Turn the duck onto its side. Pull the ends of the string firmly together and tie them securely.

6 Turn the duck breast-side up. Tuck the tail into the cavity of the bird and fold over the top skin. Push the needle through the skin.

7 Loop the string around one of the drumsticks, under the breastbone and over the other drumstick. Tie the ends of string together.

2 ROAST THE DUCK

Fat rendered from duck during cooking is discarded ———

1 Heat the oven to 220°C (425°F, Gas 7). Heat the oil in the roasting tin. Set the duck on one side and roast in the oven, 15 minutes. Turn the duck onto the opposite side and roast, another 15 minutes.

2 Spoon the fat from the roasting tin with the metal spoon and discard it.

3 Prick the duck skin all over to release the melted fat. Lower the temperature to 190°C (375°F, Gas 5). Turn the duck onto its breast, and roast it, 15 minutes longer. Discard any more melted fat.

Use 2-pronged ——— fork to prick duck skin

4 Finally, set the duck on its back and continue roasting until the juices from the cavity run clear, 15–20 minutes longer. Lift the duck with the 2-pronged fork and tip it to see the colour of the juices. Transfer the duck to a warmed platter and cover with foil to keep warm. Meanwhile, prepare the ingredients for the sauce.

3 PREPARE THE CARAMEL VINEGAR AND THE CHERRIES

1 Put the water and sugar into the small heavy-based saucepan and heat gently until the sugar is dissolved, stirring occasionally.

2 Increase the heat and boil, without stirring, until the syrup starts to turn golden around the edge, 5–8 minutes. Lower the heat and cook to a deep golden caramel, 30–60 seconds. Remove the saucepan from the heat and let the bubbles subside.

3 Pour in the vinegar. Simmer, stirring occasionally, until the caramel is dissolved and the mixture is reduced by half, 3–5 minutes. Remove from the heat and set aside.

! TAKE CARE !
The caramel will splutter when the vinegar is added and the fumes will be strong; stand at arm's length when pouring the vinegar into the saucepan.

4 Discard any cherry stalks. Stone the cherries with the cherry stoner, or scoop out the cherry stones with the tip of a vegetable peeler. Alternatively, drain the canned cherries.

Cherry stoner removes stones easily

5 In a medium saucepan, combine the caramel vinegar and the beef or veal stock.

6 Add the cherries to the pan and simmer until they are just tender, 3–5 minutes for fresh cherries, 1–2 minutes for canned. Transfer the cherries to a bowl with the slotted spoon.

4 FINISH THE SAUCE AND CARVE THE DUCK

1 Discard any fat from the roasting tin. Add the caramel vinegar and stock mixture, and bring to a boil on top of the stove, stirring to dissolve the pan juices. Simmer until the mixture is reduced by half and the liquid is well flavoured, 3–5 minutes.

2 Strain the liquid back into the saucepan. With the wooden spoon, press two-thirds of the cherries through the sieve into the liquid. Add the remaining whole cherries, bring to a boil, then add salt and pepper to taste.

Cherries are puréed to thicken sauce

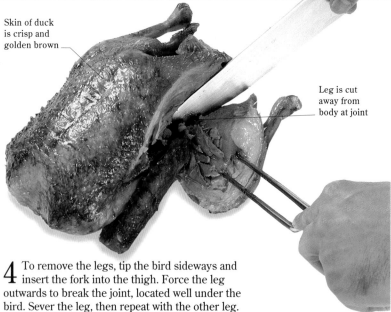

Skin of duck is crisp and golden brown

Leg is cut away from body at joint

3 Place the duck breast-side up and discard the trussing string. Hold the bird steady with the 2-pronged fork and cut the skin between the legs and body, forcing the legs outwards with the flat of the knife so the breast meat is revealed.

4 To remove the legs, tip the bird sideways and insert the fork into the thigh. Force the leg outwards to break the joint, located well under the bird. Sever the leg, then repeat with the other leg.

6 To carve the breast, cut horizontally, just above the wing joint, through the breast meat to the bone, steadying the bird with the fork.

5 Halve the leg by cutting through the joint, using the line of white fat as a guide.

Use sharp knife for carving duck

7 Cut long needle-shaped strips of breast meat, working the full length of the carcass, parallel to the rib cage.

ANNE SAYS
"Duck wing bones have no meat and are not normally served."

8 Arrange the slices of breast meat in a fan shape at one end of a warmed serving platter and the leg pieces at the other. Spoon some of the cherry sauce over the duck.

🍽 TO SERVE

Decorate the duck with a bouquet of watercress, if you like, and serve at once. Serve the remaining sauce separately.

Crisp duck and tart cherries make a delicious combination

VARIATION

DUCK WITH PEARS
CANARD AUX POIRES

Pears add a mellow sweetness to this version of Sweet-Sour Duck. The pears are poached in a red wine syrup and a few are added to the sauce to thicken it.

1 Omit the cherries and beef or veal stock. Truss and roast the duck and make the caramel vinegar as directed. Combine the caramel vinegar with 375 ml (12 fl oz) red wine in a medium saucepan.

2 Meanwhile, peel 4 small pears (total weight about 625 g/1¼ lb) with a vegetable peeler, then cut out the flower and stalk ends with a small knife. Cut each pear into quarters and scoop out the cores. At once immerse the pear quarters in the red wine mixture. Set a heatproof plate on top so the pears are completely immersed. Bring to a boil and simmer the pears until tender when tested with the tip of a knife, 8–10 minutes. Remove the pears with a slotted spoon.

3 Make the sauce, pressing 8 pear quarters through a sieve. Finish as directed, arranging a portion of leg and breast meat and 2–3 pear quarters on warmed individual plates. Spoon the sauce over the duck, and decorate with parsley sprigs, if you like.

GETTING AHEAD

The caramel vinegar and cherries can be prepared up to 12 hours ahead and kept covered. The duck is best roasted just before serving, so the skin is crisp and golden.

POUSSINS IN VINE LEAVES

Coquelets à la Vigneronne

🍽 SERVES 4　　🥣 WORK TIME 45–50 MINUTES　　🍲 COOKING TIME 60–80 MINUTES

EQUIPMENT

wooden spoon

chef's knife

2-pronged fork

food processor

ladle

large metal spoon

slotted spoon

frying pans

palette knife

small knife

bowls

kitchen string

aluminium foil

colander

large casserole with lid

paper towels

serrated knife

metal skewer

sieve

Here, small birds are doubly linked to the vineyard, with a wrapping of vine leaves to keep them moist, and white wine in the accompanying sauce.

GETTING AHEAD

The poussins can be cooked 1 day ahead and kept, covered, in the refrigerator. Reheat them in a low oven and make the sauce just before serving.

metric	SHOPPING LIST	imperial
4	poussins, each weighing about 500 g (1 lb)	4
8–12	preserved vine leaves	8–12
4	bacon rashers	4
60 ml	vegetable oil	4 tbsp
4	slices of white bread	4
30 g	butter	1 oz
15 ml	brandy	1 tbsp
250 ml	dry white wine	8 fl oz
250 ml	chicken stock (see box, page 123)	8 fl oz
	salt and pepper	
	For the stuffing	
1	shallot	1
4	slices of white bread	4
3–5	sprigs of fresh tarragon	3–5
3–5	sprigs of parsley	3–5
2	bacon rashers	2
1	chicken liver, weighing about 30 g (1 oz)	1
15 ml	brandy	1 tbsp
1	pinch of ground allspice	1

INGREDIENTS

poussins

chicken liver

bacon rashers

vine leaves

vegetable oil

dry white wine

parsley

chicken stock

butter

white bread

shallot

brandy

fresh tarragon

ground allspice

ORDER OF WORK

1 MAKE THE STUFFING

2 STUFF AND TIE THE POUSSINS

3 COOK THE POUSSINS AND FRY THE CROUTES

1 MAKE THE STUFFING

HOW TO CHOP HERBS

Parsley, dill, tarragon, rosemary, chives, thyme, and basil are herbs that are usually chopped before being added to other ingredients in a recipe. Delicate herbs such as tarragon and basil are easily bruised, so take care not to chop them too finely.

Papery skin is discarded from shallot

1 Peel the shallot, leaving a little of the root attached. Cut it in half. Set each half, flat-side down, on a chopping board. Slice horizontally, then vertically, towards the root, leaving the root end uncut. Cut across into fine dice.

1 Strip the leaves or sprigs from the stalks of the herbs, then pile the leaves or sprigs on a chopping board.

2 Trim and discard the crusts from the bread. Roughly tear the slices into pieces, and work them in the food processor to form crumbs. Chop the tarragon and parsley (see box, right).

2 Cut the leaves or sprigs into small pieces with a chef's knife. Holding the tip of the blade against the board and rocking the blade back and forth, continue chopping until the herbs are coarse or fine, as you wish.

ANNE SAYS
" *Make sure that your knife is very sharp, otherwise you will bruise the herbs rather than cut them.***"**

3 Stack the bacon rashers on the chopping board and cut them crossways into strips about 5 mm (1/4 inch) wide, using the chef's knife.

Bacon is cut into thin strips

4 Trim any membrane from the chicken liver with the small knife, then coarsely chop the liver.

5 Put the bacon into a small frying pan, and cook, stirring occasionally, until crisp and the fat is rendered (melted), 3–5 minutes. With the slotted spoon, transfer bacon to a bowl.

6 Add the shallot to the pan and cook until soft, 2–3 minutes. Add the chicken liver, sprinkle it with pepper, and cook, stirring, until brown, 1–2 minutes. Pour in the brandy and simmer, 1 minute.

Chopped herbs add colour to stuffing

7 Combine the liver mixture with the bacon. Stir in the breadcrumbs, herbs, and allspice. Season the stuffing with pepper to taste; salt may not be needed as the bacon is salty.

2 STUFF AND TIE THE POUSSINS

Good birds have plump breast and unbroken skin with no dark patches

Stuffing is loosely packed into cavity

Herbs and bacon make tasty stuffing

1 Wipe the insides of the poussins with paper towels, and season them inside and out with salt and pepper. Spoon one-quarter of the stuffing into the cavity of each bird.

3 Wrap 2 or 3 vine leaves over the breast of each poussin, then top with a folded slice of bacon. Tie each poussin with string like a parcel.

Wrapping of vine leaves and bacon flavours breast meat and keeps it moist

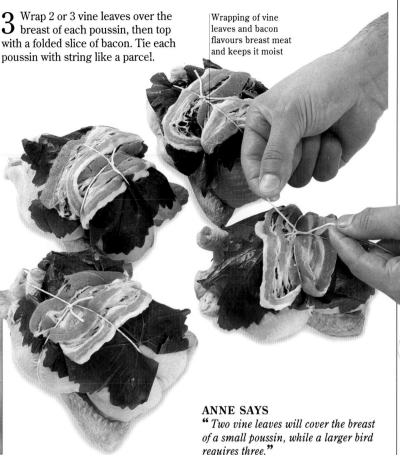

2 Rinse the vine leaves thoroughly in cold water. Drain in the colander. Place the leaves between sheets of paper towels and pat gently to dry.

ANNE SAYS
"*Two vine leaves will cover the breast of a small poussin, while a larger bird requires three.*"

3 COOK THE POUSSINS AND FRY THE CROUTES

Use skewer to check that poussins are cooked

Poussins are hard to brown all over but are cooked through during baking process

1 Heat the oven to 180°C (350°F, Gas 4). Heat half of the oil in the casserole on top of the stove. Add the poussins and brown, 5–10 minutes. Cover and transfer to the oven.

2 Bake the poussins until they are tender, and the metal skewer inserted into the stuffing for 30 seconds is hot to the touch when withdrawn, 45–55 minutes. Meanwhile, make the croûtes.

Triangles make attractive shape for croûtes

3 Cut the crusts from the slices of bread, then cut each slice in half diagonally to make 2 triangles.

4 Heat the butter with the remaining oil in a large frying pan. Add the bread triangles in batches and fry on one side until golden brown, 1–2 minutes.

5 Flip the croûtes and continue frying until golden brown on the other side, 1–2 minutes longer. Remove the croûtes from the pan and drain on paper towels.

6 Transfer the poussins to a platter. Discard the trussing strings, and cover the birds with foil to keep warm.

Scissors quickly remove trussing string

7 Using the large metal spoon, discard the fat from the casserole, then add the brandy and white wine.

8 Bring to a boil and simmer, stirring, until reduced by half, 5–7 minutes. Add the stock and reduce again by half, 5–7 minutes.

ANNE SAYS
"Be sure the wine is well reduced or the sauce will taste too strong."

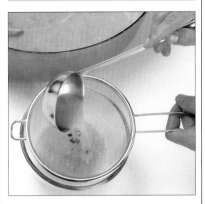

9 Using the ladle, spoon the sauce through the sieve into a small bowl. Taste for seasoning.

🍴 TO SERVE

Set the poussins on 4 warmed individual plates and spoon over the sauce. Garnish the croûtes with chopped parsley, if you like, and set 2 beside each bird. Serve at once, so that the croûtes remain crisp. Leave each guest to remove the wrapping of bacon and vine leaves.

Poussin is ideal size for individual serving

Carrot ribbons make colourful accompaniment

Chopped parsley garnish enhances croûtes

V A R I A T I O N
POUSSINS WITH BRAISED CHICORY
COQUELETS AUX ENDIVES BRAISEES

Chicory is braised at the same time as the birds in this version of Poussins in Vine Leaves. Red wine vinegar is used to deglaze the pan instead of white wine, adding a delicate tartness to the sauce.

1 Omit the vine leaves, white wine, 4 bacon rashers, the brandy from the sauce, and the bread croûtes.
2 Make the stuffing, and stuff, tie, and cook the poussins as directed. Meanwhile, braise the chicory: brush a medium baking dish with melted butter. Discard any withered outer leaves from 4 medium heads of chicory (total weight about 375 g/ 12 oz). Using a small knife, trim each head of chicory, wipe it with a paper towel, and cut it lengthways in half, through the core.

3 Arrange the chicory halves, cut-side down, in the prepared baking dish and sprinkle with salt and pepper. Butter a piece of foil and press it down on top. Bake in the oven with the poussins, turning the chicory halves once or twice until they are brown and tender when pierced with the tip of a small knife, 35–40 minutes.
4 When the poussins are cooked, remove and discard the trussing strings, and transfer the birds to 4 warmed individual plates. Arrange 2 chicory halves beside each bird, cover with foil and keep warm while finishing the sauce. Add 30 ml (2 tbsp) red wine vinegar to the casserole and stir with a wooden spoon to dissolve the pan juices. Pour in 375 ml (12 fl oz) chicken stock, add salt and pepper to taste, and simmer until the sauce is well flavoured, 3–5 minutes. Taste for seasoning, strain the sauce, and spoon it around the poussins.

SAUTE OF CHICKEN WITH PRAWNS

Sauté de Poulet aux Crevettes

 SERVES 4–6   WORK TIME 25–30 MINUTES   COOKING TIME 45–55 MINUTES

EQUIPMENT

slotted spoon

chef's knife

small knife

large sauté pan with lid

2-pronged fork

wooden spoon

saucepan

bowls

aluminium foil

chopping board

The seemingly unusual combination of chicken and shellfish is traditional in Burgundy. In this recipe, the chicken and prawns are browned, then simmered in white wine and stock. A dash of marc, *a favorite Burgundian spirit, adds rich flavour.*

metric	SHOPPING LIST	imperial
1	medium onion	1
2	shallots	2
4–6	sprigs of parsley	4–6
250 g	tomatoes	8 oz
2	garlic cloves	2
30 g	butter	1 oz
30 ml	vegetable oil	2 tbsp
375 g	raw unpeeled large prawns	12 oz
1.8 kg	chicken, cut into 8 pieces	4 lb
45 ml	marc de Bourgogne	3 tbsp
15 ml	tomato purée	1 tbsp
1	bouquet garni made with 5–6 parsley stalks, 2–3 sprigs of fresh thyme, and 1 bay leaf	1
60 ml	dry white wine	4 tbsp
125 ml	chicken stock (see box, page 123)	4 fl oz
	salt and pepper	

INGREDIENTS

chicken pieces

marc de Bourgogne†

tomato purée

raw unpeeled large prawns

parsley

garlic cloves

tomatoes

chicken stock

dry white wine

bouquet garni

shallots

butter

onion

vegetable oil

†brandy can also be used

ORDER OF WORK

1 PREPARE THE INGREDIENTS

2 COOK THE CHICKEN AND PRAWNS

1 PREPARE THE INGREDIENTS

1 Peel the onion, leaving a little of the root attached, and cut it lengthways in half. Lay each half flat and slice horizontally, then vertically, leaving the root end uncut. Finally, cut across the onion to make fine dice.

Onion skins can be used for stock

2 Peel the shallots, leaving a little of the root attached. Cut them in half, and set each half, flat-side down, on the chopping board.

3 Slice each half horizontally, then vertically, towards the root, leaving the slices attached at the root end. Cut across to make fine dice.

4 Strip the parsley leaves from the stalks. Pile the leaves on the chopping board and finely chop them. Peel, seed, and coarsely chop the tomatoes (see box, right).

Skin is easy to remove after crushing garlic clove

5 Set the flat side of the chef's knife on top of each garlic clove and strike it with your fist. Discard the skin and finely chop the cloves.

HOW TO PEEL, SEED, AND CHOP TOMATOES

Tomatoes are frequently peeled and seeded before chopping so they need not be sieved after cooking.

1 Bring a pan of water to a boil. Using a small knife, cut out the cores from the tomatoes. Score an "x" on the base of each. Immerse in the water until the skins start to split, 8–15 seconds, depending on their ripeness. Using a slotted spoon, transfer them at once to cold water to stop them cooking.

2 When cool, peel the skin from the tomatoes with a small knife. Cut them crossways in half and squeeze out the seeds.

3 Set each tomato half cut-side down and slice it. Give it a half turn and slice again. Chop the flesh coarsely or finely, as required.

2 COOK THE CHICKEN AND PRAWNS

1 Heat the butter and oil in the large sauté pan. Add the prawns and sauté over high heat, stirring occasionally, until the prawns turn pink and begin to lose their transparency, 2–3 minutes. Remove them with the slotted spoon and set aside on a plate.

Prawns turn pink as they cook

2 Season the chicken pieces with salt and pepper and add them to the pan, skin-side down. Brown the chicken well over medium heat, 8–10 minutes.

3 Using the 2-pronged fork, turn the chicken pieces over and brown the other side, 3–5 minutes.

4 Add the onion, shallots, and garlic, letting them fall to the bottom of the pan. Cover the pan, and cook over low heat until the vegetables are tender but not browned, 10 minutes.

Stock is added after solid ingredients

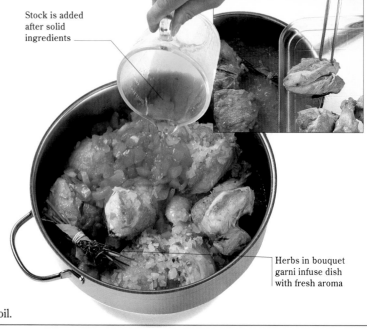

Herbs in bouquet garni infuse dish with fresh aroma

5 Pour in the marc de Bourgogne and bring to a boil. Hold a lighted match to the side of the pan to set the alcohol alight. Baste the chicken until the flames subside, 20–30 seconds.

6 Add the tomatoes, tomato purée, bouquet garni, wine, stock, and salt and pepper, stir well, and bring to a boil. Cover and simmer, turning the chicken occasionally, until tender when pierced with a fork, 10–15 minutes. Transfer the chicken to a plate and cover with foil.

7 Return the sauce to the heat, bring to a boil, and simmer until thickened slightly, 8–10 minutes.

8 Peel the shells from the prawns, leaving the tail shells intact. Transfer the prawns to a bowl.

9 Return the chicken and prawns to the pan and reheat them, stirring, 1–2 minutes. Discard the bouquet garni and taste the sauce for seasoning.

🍽 TO SERVE

Arrange the chicken pieces and prawns on a warmed platter. Spoon the sauce over the chicken and prawns, sprinkle with the chopped parsley, and serve at once.

Prawns are decoratively arranged on top of chicken pieces

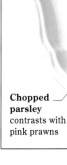

Chopped parsley contrasts with pink prawns

VARIATION

SAUTE OF CHICKEN WITH FENNEL

SAUTE DE POULET AU FENOUIL

Fresh fennel adds a hint of aniseed to this chicken casserole.

1 Omit the parsley, prawns, and marc de Bourgogne. Prepare the onion, shallots, tomatoes, and garlic as directed. Slice 2 large fennel bulbs (total weight about 750 g/1½ lb): trim the stalks and roots, discarding any tough outer pieces from the bulbs. Reserve a few of the fennel fronds for garnish. Cut the bulbs in half, then set the halves, flat-side down, on the chopping board and cut them across into thin slices.

2 Brown the chicken as directed. Transfer the chicken to a plate. Add the fennel to the pan with the onions, shallots, and garlic and cook until soft, 3–5 minutes. Return the chicken to the pan, cover, and cook, 10 minutes longer. Add 30 ml (2 tbsp) pastis or other aniseed-flavoured liqueur and flame the chicken. Add the tomatoes, tomato purée, wine, stock, and bouquet garni. Cook and finish the dish as directed. Decorate the chicken with the reserved fennel fronds.

GETTING AHEAD

The complete dish can be made up to 1 day ahead and kept, covered, in the refrigerator. Reheat it on top of the stove just before serving.

RABBIT WITH PROVENÇAL HERBS AND BAKED TOMATOES

Lapin aux Herbes de Provence, Tomates au Four

 SERVES 4   WORK TIME 35–40 MINUTES   COOKING TIME 3–3½ HOURS

EQUIPMENT

chef's knife

shallow non-metallic dish

boning knife

2-pronged fork

cleaver

large plate

pastry brush

wooden spoon   small knife

palette knife

aluminium foil

casserole with lid

bowls

chopping board

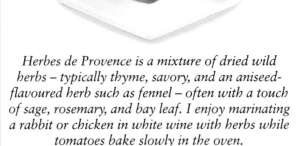

Herbes de Provence is a mixture of dried wild herbs – typically thyme, savory, and an aniseed-flavoured herb such as fennel – often with a touch of sage, rosemary, and bay leaf. I enjoy marinating a rabbit or chicken in white wine with herbs while tomatoes bake slowly in the oven.

GETTING AHEAD

The rabbit stew and the tomatoes can be cooked up to 2 days ahead and kept, covered, in the refrigerator. Warm them in a 180°C (350°F, Gas 4) oven for about 20 minutes.

metric	SHOPPING LIST	imperial
1	rabbit, weighing about 1.4 kg (3 lb)	1
2	shallots	2
250 ml	dry white wine	8 fl oz
60 ml	olive oil	4 tbsp
30 ml	herbes de Provence	2 tbsp
15 ml	plain flour	1 tbsp
250 ml	chicken stock (see box, page 123)	8 fl oz
5–7	sprigs of fresh thyme	5–7
	For the baked tomatoes	
15 ml	olive oil, more for grill rack	1 tbsp
6	plum tomatoes, total weight about 500 g (1 lb)	6
	salt and pepper	

INGREDIENTS

rabbit   herbes de Provence

chicken stock   plain flour

plum tomatoes   shallots   dry white wine

fresh thyme

olive oil

ANNE SAYS

"Herbes de Provence is available in the herbs and spices section of most good supermarkets."

ORDER OF WORK

1   **CUT UP AND MARINATE THE RABBIT**

2   **PREPARE AND BAKE THE TOMATOES**

3   **COOK THE RABBIT**

1 CUT UP AND MARINATE THE RABBIT

1 Using the boning knife, cut the front and hind leg sections from the rabbit, forcing the legs outwards, and cutting through the joints. With the cleaver, cut the back crossways into 4 pieces.

Use cleaver to cut through heavy backbone

Rabbit pieces are even in size

2 Peel and chop the shallots (see box, right). Combine the white wine, half of the oil, the shallots, and herbes de Provence in the shallow non-metallic dish.

3 Add the rabbit pieces and turn until coated. Cover, and let marinate in the refrigerator, 2–3 hours. Meanwhile, prepare and bake the tomatoes.

Turn rabbit pieces once or twice during marinating

HOW TO CHOP A SHALLOT

For a standard chop, make slices that are about 3 mm (1/8 inch) thick. For a fine chop, make the slices as thin as possible.

1 Peel the outer, papery skin from the shallot. If necessary, separate the shallot into sections at the root and peel the sections. Set the shallot or section on a chopping board, hold it steady with your fingers, and slice horizontally towards the root, leaving the slices attached at the root end.

2 Slice vertically through the shallot, again leaving the root end uncut.

3 Cut across the shallot to make fine dice. Continue chopping, if necessary, until dice are very fine.

2 PREPARE AND BAKE THE TOMATOES

1 Heat the oven to 130°C (250°F, Gas 1/2). Brush a grill rack with oil. Core the tomatoes and cut each one lengthways into 3 thick slices.

2 In a bowl, combine the tomatoes with the olive oil and salt and pepper. Toss until the tomatoes are coated.

3 Arrange the tomato slices on the grill rack, and bake them in the heated oven until most of their moisture has evaporated and they are slightly shrivelled, 2–2½ hours. Transfer them to a plate and cover with aluminium foil. Increase the oven temperature to 190°C (375°F, Gas 5).

Tomatoes should look slightly shrivelled

Use palette knife to transfer tomato slices

3 COOK THE RABBIT

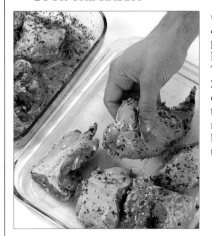

2 Heat half of the remaining oil in the casserole. Add half of the rabbit pieces and cook them over medium heat until browned, about 5 minutes. Turn the pieces with the 2-pronged fork and brown the other side. Transfer them to the plate, add the remaining oil, and brown the rest of the rabbit pieces.

1 Transfer the rabbit from the marinade to a large plate, and reserve the marinade. Season the rabbit pieces with salt and pepper.

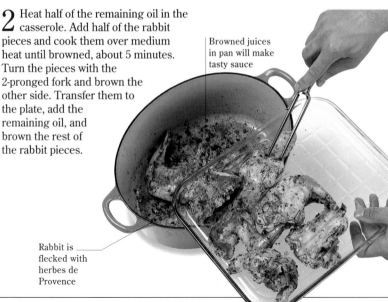

Browned juices in pan will make tasty sauce

Rabbit is flecked with herbes de Provence

3 Return all of the pieces of rabbit to the casserole and sprinkle them with the flour. Turn the rabbit pieces and cook until the flour is absorbed, 2–3 minutes.

Rabbit pieces cook in stock and rich marinade

4 Pour in the reserved marinade and the stock, and stir to mix with the rabbit. Cover, and bake, stirring occasionally, until the rabbit is very tender, 50–55 minutes. Return the tomatoes to the oven for the last 10 minutes of cooking time to heat through separately, if you like. Strip the thyme leaves from half of the stems.

 TO SERVE

Arrange a rabbit leg and a piece of back meat on each of 4 warmed plates. Spoon the sauce over the rabbit and place the baked tomatoes alongside. Garnish with fresh thyme leaves and sprigs.

Herbed sauce is aromatic accompaniment for braised rabbit

Ruby tomatoes are tender and smoky in flavour from long, slow baking

VARIATION

CHICKEN WITH PROVENÇAL HERBS AND GARLIC POTATOES

POULET AUX HERBES DE PROVENCE, POMMES A L'AIL

Chicken replaces the rabbit in this stew, which is served with baked garlic potatoes.

1 Omit the rabbit and baked tomatoes. Chop 4 garlic cloves: lightly crush each one with the flat of a knife. Discard the skin and finely chop the cloves. Make the marinade as directed, adding half of the chopped garlic. Cut 1 chicken (weighing about 1.8 kg/4 lb) into 8 pieces and marinate as for the rabbit.

2 While the chicken is marinating, prepare the potatoes: scrub 750 g (1½ lb) new potatoes under cold running water, but do not peel. Cut each potato lengthways into 5 mm (¼ inch) slices. Put them into a bowl, add the remaining garlic, 30 ml (2 tbsp) olive oil, and salt and pepper. Toss the potatoes until coated, then spread on a baking sheet so that each slice lies flat.

3 Heat the oven to 190°C (375°F, Gas 5). Brown and bake the chicken as directed for the rabbit, allowing the same cooking time. While the chicken is cooking, bake the potatoes in the bottom third of the oven until they begin to turn golden, about 20 minutes. Turn them and continue baking until the potato slices are brown and crispy, 20 minutes longer.

CASSOULET WITH QUICK CONFIT

 SERVES 8   WORK TIME 50–55 MINUTES*   COOKING TIME 1¾–2¼ HOURS

EQUIPMENT

large flameproof
casserole with lid

colander

cling film

paper towels

2-pronged fork

chef's knife

bowls,
1 non-metallic

boning knife

slotted spoon

small knife

large metal spoon

wooden
spoon

heavy-duty
plastic bag

metal skewer

saucepans

rolling pin

poultry shears

chopping board

A traditional cassoulet is a slowly cooked feast of beans, confit of preserved duck or goose, and a variety of meats and sausages. Here I show you an equally delicious version, using a speedy confit, which takes a quarter of the usual time.

plus 8–12 hours marinating time

metric	SHOPPING LIST	imperial
250 g	streaky bacon rashers	8 oz
750 g	boneless lamb shoulder	1½ lb
4	garlic cloves	4
1 kg	tomatoes	2 lb
375 g	onions	12 oz
375 g	pork sausages	12 oz
175 ml	dry white wine	6 fl oz
1.5 litres	veal stock (see box, page 123) or water	2⅓ pints
1	bouquet garni made with 5–6 parsley stalks, 2–3 sprigs of fresh thyme, and 1 bay leaf	1
15 ml	tomato purée	1 tbsp
375 g	garlic poaching sausages	12 oz
4 cans	white beans, each weighing 400 g (14 oz)	4 cans
60 g	dried breadcrumbs	2 oz
	salt and pepper	
	For the quick duck confit	
1	duck, weighing about 1.8 kg (4 lb)	1
5 ml	black peppercorns	1 tsp
3–5	sprigs of fresh thyme	3–5
3	bay leaves	3
45 ml	coarse or kosher salt	3 tbsp
15 ml	vegetable oil	1 tbsp
15 g	butter	½ oz

INGREDIENTS

lamb shoulder

duck

tomato purée

veal stock

pork
sausages

dry
white
wine

bouquet
garni

garlic
cloves

poaching
sausages

onions

streaky
bacon rashers

vegetable
oil

tomatoes

butter

black
peppercorns

canned
white beans

fresh herbs

dried
breadcrumbs

ORDER OF WORK

1 CUT UP THE DUCK

2 MAKE THE QUICK DUCK CONFIT

3 PREPARE OTHER INGREDIENTS

4 COOK THE MEATS, ASSEMBLE, AND BAKE THE CASSOULET

1 CUT UP THE DUCK

1 Trim the excess fat and skin from the duck. Using the boning knife, cut down between one leg and the body of the duck. Twist the leg sharply outwards to break the joint, cut through it, and cut the whole leg from the body. Repeat with the other leg.

> Boning knife should cut easily through joint

2 Cut each leg in half at the joint between the thigh and the drumstick, using the line of white fat on the underside as a guide.

3 Slit closely along both sides of the breastbone to loosen the skin and meat from the bone. With the poultry shears or the chef's knife, cut along the breastbone to split it lengthways in half.

4 Turn the duck over. Cut away the rib bones and backbone from the breast in one piece, leaving the breast pieces with the wing joints attached. Discard the back and rib bones.

5 Cut each breast piece diagonally in half, cutting through the bones so that a portion of the breast meat is left attached to the wing joint. Cut off any sharp bones.

ANNE SAYS
"You can ask your butcher to joint the duck for you, but the backbone may be included. Be sure to remove it."

2 MAKE THE QUICK DUCK CONFIT

Duck is rubbed with coarse-grained salt

1 Put the peppercorns into the plastic bag and crush them with the rolling pin. Strip the thyme leaves from the stalks. Crush the bay leaves with your fingers. Combine the peppercorns, thyme, and bay leaves in a bowl.

2 Rub each piece of duck with some of the coarse salt, and put the pieces into the non-metallic bowl. Sprinkle the duck pieces with the peppercorn mixture. Cover with cling film, and leave to marinate in the refrigerator, 8–12 hours.

3 Rinse the duck pieces with cold water, then wipe them with paper towels. Heat the oil and butter in the casserole. Add the duck pieces to the casserole, skin-side down, and brown them well over low heat so the fat is thoroughly melted, 20–25 minutes. Turn the pieces using the 2-pronged fork and brown the other side more quickly, about 5 minutes. Transfer to a plate and set aside.

4 Spoon all but 30 ml (2 tbsp) of fat from the casserole into a small bowl and discard it. Set the casserole aside for the cassoulet. Meanwhile, prepare the other ingredients.

3 PREPARE OTHER INGREDIENTS

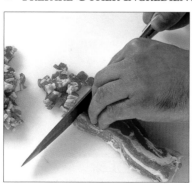

1 Stack the bacon rashers on the chopping board. Cut crossways into strips with the chef's knife.

2 Trim the excess fat and sinew from the lamb shoulder, then cut the meat into 5 cm (2 inch) cubes.

3 Set the flat side of the chef's knife on top of each garlic clove and strike it with your fist. Discard the skin and finely chop the cloves.

4 Core the tomatoes. Score an "x" on the bases. Immerse in boiling water until skins split, 8–15 seconds. Transfer to cold water. When cool, peel.

5 Cut the tomatoes crossways in half, squeeze out the seeds, then coarsely chop each half. Peel, trim, and chop the onions (see box, below).

HOW TO CHOP AN ONION

The size of dice when chopping an onion depends on the thickness of the initial slices. For a standard size, make slices 5 mm (1/4 inch) thick. For finely chopped onions, slice very thinly.

1 Peel the onion and trim the top; leave a little of the root attached.

2 Cut the onion lengthways in half, through root and stalk.

3 Put one half, cut-side down, on the chopping board and hold the onion steady with one hand. Using a chef's knife, make a series of horizontal cuts from the top towards the root but not through it.

4 Make a series of lengthways vertical cuts, cutting just to the root but not through it.

ANNE SAYS
"When slicing, tuck your fingertips under and use your knuckles to guide the blade of the knife."

5 Slice the onion crossways into dice. For finely chopped onion, continue chopping until you have the fineness required.

Cut across at even intervals for neat dice

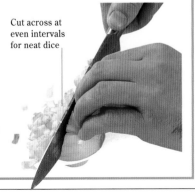

4 COOK THE MEATS, ASSEMBLE, AND BAKE THE CASSOULET

1 Heat the oven to 190°C (375°F, Gas 5). Heat the casserole with the reserved duck fat, add the bacon, and fry, stirring, until the fat is rendered (melted), 3–5 minutes. Transfer the bacon to a bowl with the slotted spoon.

2 Season the lamb with salt and pepper. Add the lamb in batches to the casserole and cook over high heat, stirring occasionally, until evenly browned, 3–5 minutes. With the slotted spoon, transfer the lamb to the bowl.

3 Add the pork sausages to the casserole and brown them all over. Transfer the sausages to a plate. Discard all but 30 ml (2 tbsp) fat from the casserole. Add the onions and cook until soft, 3–5 minutes.

4 Return the lamb to the casserole with the bacon and duck confit. Add the tomatoes, white wine, and two-thirds of the stock, and stir to dissolve the pan juices.

5 Stir in the chopped garlic, bouquet garni, tomato purée, and salt and pepper. Bring to a boil on top of the stove, skimming occasionally. Cover the casserole and bake in the heated oven until the meat is almost tender, 1–1¼ hours.

ANNE SAYS
"If the meats seem dry during cooking, add more stock or water."

6 Meanwhile, put the poaching sausages into a pan with water to cover. Bring just to a boil. Simmer very gently until the skewer inserted in a sausage is warm to the touch, 20–25 minutes. Do not boil or the sausages will burst.

7 Drain the sausages and let cool until tepid. Slit the skins with the small knife, then peel the sausages and cut them crossways into 2 cm (³/₄ inch) slices.

8 Drain the beans in the colander. Rinse with cold water, and drain them again thoroughly.

9 Add both kinds of sausage and the beans to the casserole. Stir to mix, and bring just to a boil on top of the stove. The cassoulet should be very moist but not soupy. If necessary, add more stock or water. Discard the bouquet garni and taste for seasoning.

10 Sprinkle with the breadcrumbs and return to the oven. Bake, uncovered, until a golden crust forms on top and the lamb is tender, 20–25 minutes.

ANNE SAYS
"If you like, grill the casserole for 2–3 minutes to brown the breadcrumbs further."

¶◉¶ TO SERVE
Serve the cassoulet directly from the casserole, giving each diner a combination of lamb, duck, and sausages. Sprinkle with chopped parsley, if you like.

Chopped parsley contrasts with meats and sausages

VARIATION
POOR MAN'S CASSOULET
In this version of cassoulet, the duck is omitted and pork replaces the lamb. Preparation is even less work, and the dish costs less too!

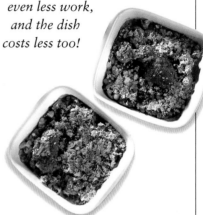

1 Omit the quick confit and lamb. Cut 750 g (1½ lb) boneless pork shoulder into cubes as for the lamb. Prepare the bacon, garlic, tomatoes, and onions as directed.
2 Cook the bacon and pork as directed. Assemble and bake the cassoulet as directed, cooking both kinds of sausages and adding them with the beans. Discard the bouquet garni and taste for seasoning. Divide the cassoulet between 8 individual ovenproof dishes, sprinkle with breadcrumbs, and bake, 15–20 minutes. Sprinkle the cassoulet with chopped parsley, if you like, and serve very hot, in the dishes.

─ **GETTING AHEAD** ─
The cassoulet can be made up to 2 days ahead and the flavours will mellow. Keep it, covered, in the refrigerator and reheat it on top of the stove, adding a little water to thin it if necessary.

SPRING LAMB STEW

Navarin Printanier

EQUIPMENT

round casserole
with lid

medium
saucepan

bowls

boning knife

colander

chef's knife

small knife

sieve

wooden spoon

slotted spoon

vegetable peeler

ladle

chopping board

*The vivid flavours of young lamb and baby
vegetables show at their best in this colourful stew.
The secret is to simmer the lamb so that it is soft
enough to fall from a fork, while only lightly
cooking the vegetables.*

GETTING AHEAD

The stew can be made up to 2 days ahead and kept, covered,
in the refrigerator. Reheat it on top of the stove.

metric	SHOPPING LIST	imperial
750 g	boneless lamb shoulder	1¹/₂ lb
2	garlic cloves	2
500 g	baby onions	1 lb
30 ml	vegetable oil	2 tbsp
30 ml	plain flour	2 tbsp
15 ml	tomato purée	1 tbsp
1	bouquet garni made with 5–6 parsley stalks, 2–3 sprigs of fresh thyme, and 1 bay leaf	1
500 ml	veal stock (see box, page 123), more if needed	16 fl oz
375 g	tomatoes	12 oz
250 g	baby carrots or medium carrots	8 oz
250 g	turnips	8 oz
250 g	French beans	8 oz
750 g	small new potatoes	1¹/₂ lb
4–5	sprigs of parsley	4–5
150 g	fresh or frozen peas	5 oz
	salt and pepper	

INGREDIENTS

 boneless lamb shoulder

vegetable
oil

 carrots

 tomatoes

 garlic
cloves

 veal stock

baby onions

 French beans   parsley

 turnips

 peas

 new potatoes

 plain flour

 tomato purée

 bouquet garni

ORDER OF WORK

1 PREPARE AND
   SIMMER THE LAMB

2 PREPARE THE
   VEGETABLES

3 FINISH THE STEW

1 PREPARE AND SIMMER THE LAMB

1 Using the boning knife, trim any fat and sinew from the lamb, then cut it into 2.5–4 cm (1–1¹/₂ inch) cubes.

Baby onions remain firm after blanching and peeling

3 Put the baby onions into a bowl, pour over boiling water to cover, and let stand, 2 minutes. Drain the onions, then peel them, leaving a little of the root to hold them together. Heat the oil in the casserole. Add the onions and cook, stirring occasionally, until golden, 5–7 minutes. Remove with the slotted spoon and set aside.

2 Set the flat side of the chef's knife on top of each garlic clove and strike it with your fist. Discard the skin and finely chop the cloves, moving the knife blade back and forth.

4 Season the lamb cubes with salt and pepper, and add to the casserole, in batches if necessary. Cook over high heat, stirring occasionally, until evenly browned, 3–5 minutes. With the slotted spoon, transfer the lamb to a bowl.

5 Return all the cooked lamb to the pan, sprinkle with the flour, then stir to mix. Cook over medium heat, stirring occasionally, until the flour is browned, 2–3 minutes.

6 Let the casserole cool slightly, then stir in the tomato purée, chopped garlic, and bouquet garni. Pour in enough stock to just cover the meat, stir to mix, and bring to a boil. Cover, and simmer, 1 hour. Meanwhile, prepare the vegetables.

2 PREPARE THE VEGETABLES

1 Core the tomatoes and score an "x" on the base of each one. Immerse the tomatoes in boiling water until the skins start to split, 8–15 seconds depending on their ripeness. Using the slotted spoon, transfer the tomatoes at once to a bowl of cold water.

2 When cool, peel the skins off the tomatoes. Cut the tomatoes crossways in half, squeeze out the seeds, then coarsely chop each tomato half.

3 If the baby carrots have green tops, trim them, leaving a little of the green, then scrape to remove the thin skin. If using medium carrots, peel them, then quarter lengthways.

Baby carrots look neat when green tops remain

4 With the vegetable peeler, peel the turnips. Cut them into quarters or 6 or 8 wedges, depending on their size, and trim off the sharp edges with the small knife.

Beans are cut on diagonal for attractive presentation

5 With your fingers, snap the ends off the beans. Cut the beans into 2.5 cm (1 inch) pieces.

6 Peel the potatoes with the small knife and put them into a bowl of cold water to prevent discoloration.

7 Strip the parsley leaves from the stalks, pile the leaves on the chopping board, and finely chop them.

3 FINISH THE STEW

1 With the slotted spoon, transfer the meat to a large bowl, then skim the fat from the sauce. Strain the sauce over the meat, then return the meat and sauce to the casserole. Taste the sauce for seasoning.

2 Drain the potatoes, and add to the casserole with the turnips, onions, tomatoes, and carrots. Pour in stock to almost cover the meat and vegetables. Cover, and simmer, 20–25 minutes.

3 Add the peas and beans and simmer until the lamb and vegetables are tender, 25–30 minutes longer. Taste for seasoning.

ANNE SAYS
" *The sauce should be glossy and lightly thickened. If it is thin, remove the lid when adding the peas and beans so the sauce reduces.* "

🍽 TO SERVE
Ladle the stew onto warmed plates and sprinkle with the chopped parsley.

Assortment of baby vegetables adds colour to lamb stew

Lamb cubes are meltingly tender

VARIATION
LAMB RATATOUILLE
RATATOUILLE D'AGNEAU
Here, ratatouille is cooked with lamb to make a tasty stew.

1 Omit the baby onions, tomato purée, bouquet garni, carrots, turnips, French beans, potatoes, parsley, and peas. Brown the lamb as directed, using olive oil instead of vegetable oil, then add the stock and simmer, 1¼ hours. Meanwhile, prepare the vegetables.
2 Trim 1 aubergine (weighing about 500 g/1 lb) and cut it lengthways in half. Cut each half lengthways into 4–5 strips, then cut across into 2.5 cm (1 inch) chunks. Put into a colander and sprinkle with salt. Let stand, 30 minutes. Meanwhile, chop 3 garlic cloves. Peel, seed, and chop 500 g (1 lb) tomatoes. Core 1 green and 1 red pepper. Halve the peppers and scrape out the seeds and ribs. Set each half cut-side down, flatten it, and slice it lengthways into thin strips.
3 Peel and thinly slice 1 large onion. Rinse the aubergine chunks and pat dry on paper towels.
4 Heat 45 ml (3 tbsp) olive oil in a frying pan. Add the onions and garlic and cook, stirring, until soft, 3–5 minutes. Stir in the pepper strips and cook, 2–3 minutes. Add the aubergine, salt and pepper, and cook, stirring, until the vegetables are just tender, 7–10 minutes. Add the tomatoes.
5 Add the vegetables and 125 ml (4 fl oz) veal stock to the lamb. Cook covered, 15 minutes, then cook uncovered, until the lamb and vegetables are tender and the sauce well flavoured, 20 minutes longer. Taste for seasoning, garnish, and serve.

LEG OF LAMB WITH ROASTED GARLIC AND SHALLOTS

Gigot à l'Ail et aux Echalotes Rôtis

 SERVES 8   WORK TIME 15–20 MINUTES   COOKING TIME 1¼–2 HOURS

EQUIPMENT

boning knife

small knife

shallow roasting tin

metal spoon

2-pronged fork

carving knife

metal skewer†

aluminium foil

wooden spoon

slotted spoon

chopping board

†meat thermometer can also be used

The flavours of garlic and shallots sweeten and mellow when they are slowly roasted in their skins. Here, they are cooked with a leg of lamb and softened to a purée that is delicious spread directly on the meat, or on a piece of crusty baguette.

GETTING AHEAD

In this simple recipe, the lamb and vegetables are best roasted just before serving.

metric	SHOPPING LIST	imperial
1	small leg of lamb, weighing about 2.25 kg (5 lb)	1
2	heads of garlic	2
500 g	shallots	1 lb
5–7	sprigs of fresh thyme	5–7
30 ml	olive oil	2 tbsp
	salt and pepper	
125 ml	water, more if needed	4 fl oz
125 ml	dry white wine	4 fl oz
250 ml	beef or veal stock (see box, page 123)	8 fl oz
1	small bunch of watercress for decoration	1

INGREDIENTS

leg of lamb

garlic

shallots

fresh thyme   watercress

beef stock

dry white wine

olive oil†

†vegetable oil can also be used

ORDER OF WORK

1 PREPARE THE INGREDIENTS

2 ROAST THE LAMB AND VEGETABLES; FINISH THE DISH

1 PREPARE THE INGREDIENTS

1 Heat the oven to 230°C (450°F, Gas 8). Using the boning knife, trim all but a thin layer of fat from the lamb.

ANNE SAYS
"*A thin layer of fat adds flavour and helps keep the lamb moist while it is cooking.*"

Boning knife slices easily through fat

2 With the heel of your hand, press sharply down on the heads of garlic to loosen the cloves. Separate the cloves, and discard the root and any loose skin.

Outer layer of loose, papery skin is removed from garlic cloves

Tops of shallots are removed for neat presentation

Skin protects shallots during baking

3 With the small knife, trim the tops and roots from the shallots but do not peel them.

4 Strip the thyme leaves from half of the sprigs, and reserve the remaining sprigs for garnish.

2 ROAST THE LAMB AND VEGETABLES; FINISH THE DISH

1 Put the lamb into the roasting tin and spoon over the oil. Sprinkle the lamb with the thyme leaves and salt and pepper. Roast in the heated oven until browned, 10–15 minutes.

ANNE SAYS
"Cooking at high heat forms a crust on the meat and seals in the juices."

2 Lower the oven temperature to 180°C (350°F, Gas 4). Add the garlic cloves and shallots to the roasting tin with the 125 ml (4 fl oz) water, and stir to mix with the pan juices.

3 Continue cooking the lamb, basting often, and adding more water if necessary, 1–1¼ hours for rare meat or 1¼–1½ hours for medium done. When rare, the metal skewer inserted in the meat for 30 seconds will be cool to the touch when withdrawn, and a meat thermometer will show 51°C (125°F). When the meat is medium done, the skewer will be warm and a thermometer will show 60°C (140°F).

ANNE SAYS
"The garlic and shallots should be tender when pierced with the metal skewer. If necessary, continue cooking them 5–10 minutes longer."

Skewer is inserted into thickest part of leg

4 When the lamb is cooked to your taste, remove it from the tin, cover with foil, and keep warm. Remove the garlic and shallots, cover, and keep warm. Let the lamb stand 10–15 minutes before carving.

5 Meanwhile, make the gravy: discard the fat from the tin. Add the wine and bring to a boil, stirring to dissolve the pan juices. Simmer, stirring, 3–5 minutes. Stir in the stock and continue simmering until the gravy is well flavoured, 2–3 minutes longer. Taste for seasoning.

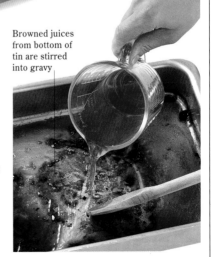

Browned juices from bottom of tin are stirred into gravy

6 Carve the meat: set the lamb, rounded-side up. Hold the leg by the shank and cut thin horizontal slices.

Lamb is carved into thin slices with sawing action

7 Turn the leg over and carve horizontal slices from the other side of the bone. Finally, carve slivers from the meat left next to the bone.

🍽 TO SERVE

Arrange the lamb, garlic, and shallots on a warmed platter. Decorate the lamb with the reserved thyme and a watercress bouquet. Serve the gravy separately.

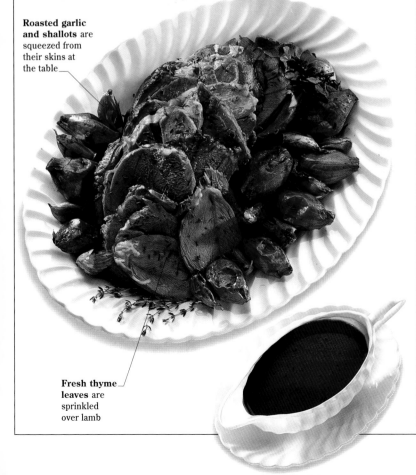

Roasted garlic and shallots are squeezed from their skins at the table

Fresh thyme leaves are sprinkled over lamb

VARIATION

LEG OF LAMB WITH POTATOES

GIGOT BOULANGERE

Boulangère *means baker's style, and, before every home had an oven, this dish would have been cooked by the local baker.*

1 Omit the shallots, water, white wine, and watercress. Trim the lamb as directed. Peel 4 garlic cloves. Finely chop 2 and cut the other 2 into thin slivers. Make several shallow incisions in the lamb and insert the slivers.

2 Peel 500 g (1 lb) onions and cut them lengthways in half. Lay each half flat and cut across into thin slices. Peel 1 kg (2 lb) potatoes, slice thinly, and put into a bowl. Strip the thyme leaves from the stalks and mix with the potatoes. Cover the potatoes with a wet cloth so that they do not discolour.

3 Heat 30 ml (2 tbsp) oil in a frying pan. Cook the onions and garlic until soft, 5–8 minutes. Stir the onions into the potatoes with a pinch of nutmeg and salt and pepper. Heat the oven to 230°C (450°F, Gas 8).

4 Brown the lamb in a shallow baking dish as directed. Transfer to a plate. Spread the potato mixture over the bottom of the dish. Add 500 ml (16 fl oz) beef or veal stock, adding more if needed so the potatoes are almost covered. Set the lamb on top, lower the heat to 180°C (350°F, Gas 4), and continue roasting as directed. If necessary, remove the lamb, keep warm, and continue baking the potato mixture until golden. Carve the lamb and serve with the potatoes and gravy.

STEAK AU POIVRE

 SERVES 4   WORK TIME 25–30 MINUTES*   COOKING TIME 10–15 MINUTES

EQUIPMENT

slotted spoon

chef's knife

small knife

large frying pan

long-handled spoon

2-pronged fork

vegetable peeler

deep-fat fryer†

bowls

colander

rolling pin

heavy-duty plastic bag

shallow non-metallic dish

aluminium foil

paper towels

chopping board

†large deep saucepan can also be used

Black peppercorns are crushed to release their flavour, then pressed onto steak which is left to marinate for up to 6 hours – the longer the marinating, the more piquant the dish. Pommes frites or French-fried potatoes are the classic complement to the intensely peppered steak and sauce.

GETTING AHEAD

The steak can be left to marinate and the potatoes cut and fried for the first time up to 6 hours ahead. Cook the steak and give the potatoes a second frying just before serving.

plus 2–6 hours marinating time

metric	SHOPPING LIST	imperial
1	sirloin steak, 5 cm (2 inches) thick, weighing about 1 kg (2 lb)	1
45 ml	black peppercorns	3 tbsp
1 kg	potatoes	2 lb
15 ml	vegetable oil, more for deep frying	1 tbsp
30 g	butter	1 oz
	salt	
125 ml	brandy	4 fl oz
125 ml	double cream	4 fl oz

INGREDIENTS

sirloin steak

brandy

double cream

butter

vegetable oil

potatoes

black peppercorns

ANNE SAYS

"Choose your favourite steak when making Steak au Poivre – large or small, with or without a bone – all are equally delicious when prepared this way."

ORDER OF WORK

1 MARINATE THE STEAK

2 PREPARE THE POTATOES AND FRY THEM FOR THE FIRST TIME

3 COOK THE STEAK, FINISH FRYING THE POTATOES, AND MAKE THE SAUCE

1 MARINATE THE STEAK

1 Trim any excess fat and sinew from the steak, leaving a thin layer of fat to flavour the meat during cooking.

2 With the small knife, slash diagonally through the fat to the beef at 4 cm (1½ inch) intervals.

ANNE SAYS

"*This diagonal slashing cuts through the membrane that lies between the fat and the beef, and prevents the steak from buckling during cooking.*"

3 Put the peppercorns into the plastic bag and crush them with the rolling pin.

Press peppercorns firmly onto both sides of meat

Peppercorns are crushed coarsely to release flavour

4 Put the steak into the shallow dish, and, with your hands, press the crushed peppercorns onto both sides of the meat. Cover, and leave to marinate in the refrigerator, 2–6 hours. Meanwhile, prepare the potatoes.

2 PREPARE THE POTATOES AND FRY THEM FOR THE FIRST TIME

Large baking potatoes make good French fries

1 Peel the potatoes. Square off the sides of each one and cut the potatoes vertically into 1 cm (³/8 inch) slices.

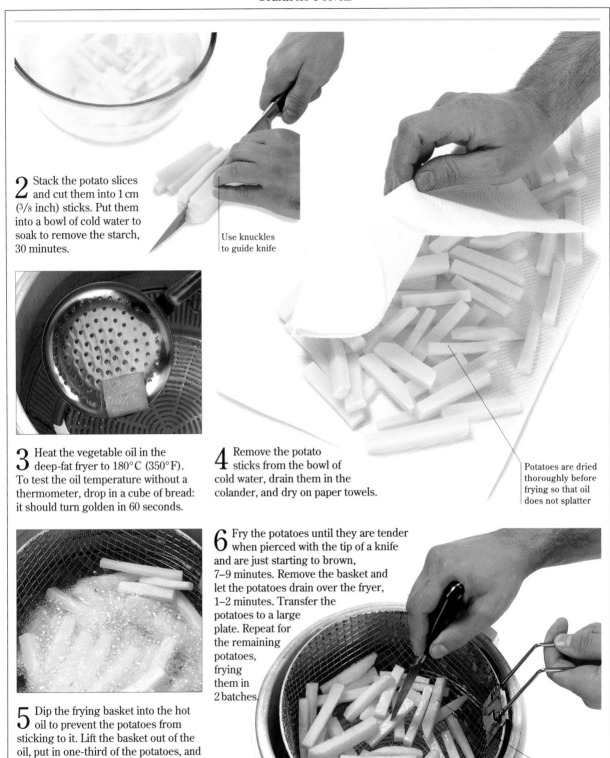

2 Stack the potato slices and cut them into 1 cm (³/₈ inch) sticks. Put them into a bowl of cold water to soak to remove the starch, 30 minutes.

Use knuckles to guide knife

3 Heat the vegetable oil in the deep-fat fryer to 180°C (350°F). To test the oil temperature without a thermometer, drop in a cube of bread: it should turn golden in 60 seconds.

4 Remove the potato sticks from the bowl of cold water, drain them in the colander, and dry on paper towels.

Potatoes are dried thoroughly before frying so that oil does not splatter

6 Fry the potatoes until they are tender when pierced with the tip of a knife and are just starting to brown, 7–9 minutes. Remove the basket and let the potatoes drain over the fryer, 1–2 minutes. Transfer the potatoes to a large plate. Repeat for the remaining potatoes, frying them in 2 batches.

5 Dip the frying basket into the hot oil to prevent the potatoes from sticking to it. Lift the basket out of the oil, put in one-third of the potatoes, and carefully lower the basket into the oil.

! TAKE CARE !
Lower potatoes gradually into hot oil.

Potatoes will brown later, during second frying

3 COOK THE STEAK, FINISH FRYING THE POTATOES, AND MAKE THE SAUCE

1 If the potatoes were fried for the first time well in advance and the oil has cooled completely, reheat the oil in the deep-fat fryer to 190°C (375°F). To test the oil temperature, drop in a cube of bread: it should turn golden in about 30 seconds.

2 Heat 15 ml (1 tbsp) vegetable oil with the butter in the large frying pan. For a mild flavour, scrape off and discard the pepper from the steak; for a stronger flavour, leave it on. Season the steak with salt. Put the steak into the pan, and fry it over high heat until brown, 4–6 minutes. Meanwhile, if the potatoes were fried for the first time not long in advance, and the oil is still warm, reheat it in the deep-fat fryer to 190°C (375°F).

! TAKE CARE !
Do not leave hot oil unattended.

Tender steak cooks quickly

3 With the 2-pronged fork, flip the steak and continue cooking until the second side is brown, 4–6 minutes longer for rare steak, or 6–8 minutes longer for medium steak.

4 To test if the steak is done, press it in the centre with your fingertip. If spongy, it is still rare; if firm, it is well done.

5 Remove the steak from the pan and cover with foil. Pour off the fat and discard.

Lift steak out of pan with 2-pronged fork

Potatoes are fried in batches so that they do not crowd pan

6 Finish frying the potatoes. Return one-third of the potatoes to the basket and lower it into the hot oil. Continue frying until crisp and golden brown, 1–2 minutes. Drain the potatoes on paper towels. Repeat with the remaining potatoes.

7 Return the cooked steak to the frying pan. Pour in the brandy and bring it to a boil.

Steak is coated with crisp peppercorn crust

Brandy is boiled before flaming to mellow flavour

8 Hold a lighted match to the side of the pan to light the brandy. Baste the steak with the pan juices until the flames subside, 20–30 seconds.

! TAKE CARE !
Flames can rise quite high, so stand well back and use a long-handled spoon for basting.

9 Transfer the steak to a carving board, and cover to keep warm. Add the cream to the frying pan and simmer, stirring to dissolve the pan juices. Taste the sauce for seasoning.

10 Trim any remaining fat from the steak, then carve the steak into diagonal slices about 2.5 cm (1 inch) thick.

🍴 TO SERVE
Divide the slices of steak among warmed individual plates and spoon the sauce on top. Sprinkle the French fries lightly with salt and pile them beside the steak.

VARIATION

STEAK WITH WHITE WINE AND SHALLOTS
STEAK AU VIN BLANC ET ECHALOTES

In this lighter version of Steak au Poivre, white wine, shallots, and herbs replace the brandy and cream.

1 Omit the brandy and double cream. Reduce the quantity of peppercorns to 15 ml (1 tbsp), and marinate 4 steaks, 2 cm (3/4 inch) thick (total weight about 1 kg/2 lb) as directed.
2 Peel 2 shallots, leaving a little of the root attached, and cut them in half. Set each half, flat-side down, on a chopping board and slice horizontally, leaving the slices attached at the root. Slice vertically, again leaving the root end uncut, then cut across the shallot to make fine dice.

3 Strip the leaves from 3–5 sprigs each of fresh tarragon, fresh thyme, and parsley. Pile the leaves on the chopping board and coarsely chop them with a chef's knife.
4 Peel the potatoes, then square off the ends and sides. Cut each one lengthways into 5 mm (1/4 inch) vertical slices. Stack the slices and cut lengthways into 5 mm (1/4 inch) sticks about 5 cm (2 inches) long; soak and dry them as directed.
5 Heat the oil in a deep-fat fryer to 180°C (350°F) and fry the potatoes for the first time as directed, 4–6 minutes. Drain on paper towels.
6 Season the steaks with salt, and fry as directed. Transfer the steaks to a plate, and cover to keep warm.
7 Pour off all but 15 ml (1 tbsp) of fat from the frying pan, and add the shallots. Cook, stirring occasionally, until soft, 2–3 minutes. Add 125 ml (4 fl oz) dry white wine to the pan, stir to dissolve the pan juices, and simmer until reduced by half, 3–4 minutes. Reheat the oil in the deep-fat fryer to 190°C (375°F) as directed. Add 250 ml (8 fl oz) beef or veal stock to the pan, and simmer again until reduced by half. Finish frying the potatoes as directed.
8 Take the pan from the heat, add the chopped herbs to the sauce, and taste for seasoning. Set the steaks on individual plates and serve with the sauce spooned on top. Sprinkle the French fries with a little salt and pile them beside the steak.

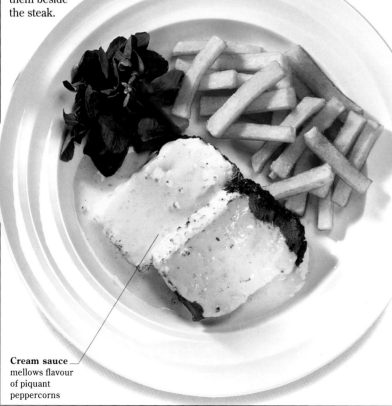

Cream sauce mellows flavour of piquant peppercorns

PORK CHOPS WITH MUSTARD SAUCE

Côtes de Porc Dijonnaise

 SERVES 4   WORK TIME 20–25 MINUTES   COOKING TIME 50–60 MINUTES

EQUIPMENT

chef's knife

slotted spoon

metal spoon

large frying pan with lid

whisk

wooden spoon

paper towels

2-pronged fork

bowls

chopping board

ANNE SAYS

"*The frying pan should hold the pork chops snugly. If the pan is too big, the simmering liquid will not cover enough of the chops and they will dry out and may become tough.*"

The fame of Dijon mustard dates back to the Middle Ages. Today strict rules ensure that it is made only from ground black mustard seeds, salt, spices, and verjuice (sour grape juice), wine, or vinegar. Such is its renown that any dish with the word Dijonnaise in its name has mustard as the principal flavouring.

GETTING AHEAD
The pork chops are best cooked just before serving.

INGREDIENTS

pork chops

bouquet garni

veal stock

streaky bacon rashers

dry white wine

parsley

butter

plain flour

double cream

Dijon mustard

metric	SHOPPING LIST	imperial
4	pork chops, each weighing about 175 g (6 oz)	4
125 g	streaky bacon rashers	4 oz
30 g	butter	1 oz
15 ml	plain flour	1 tbsp
250 ml	dry white wine	8 fl oz
250 ml	veal stock (page 123) or water, more if needed	8 fl oz
1	bouquet garni (see box, page 90)	1
5–7	sprigs of parsley	5–7
60 ml	double cream	4 tbsp
15 ml	Dijon mustard, more to taste	1 tbsp
	salt and pepper	

ORDER OF WORK

1 PREPARE THE PORK CHOPS AND MAKE THE SAUCE

2 FINISH THE DISH

1 PREPARE THE PORK CHOPS AND MAKE THE SAUCE

1 Trim the excess fat from the pork chops with the chef's knife, and sprinkle them with pepper.

Only lean meat is left when excess fat is removed

2 Stack the bacon rashers on the chopping board and cut them crossways into strips.

3 Heat the bacon in the frying pan, and cook, stirring occasionally, until crisp and the fat is rendered (melted), 3–5 minutes. With the slotted spoon, remove the bacon from the pan and drain on paper towels.

4 Discard all but 15 ml (1 tbsp) of the bacon fat. Heat the butter with the remaining bacon fat until foaming.

2-pronged fork turns chops efficiently

Chops should be well browned

5 Add the pork chops to the pan and brown them well over medium heat, about 5 minutes. Turn the chops with the 2-pronged fork and brown the other side. Remove them from the pan and set aside.

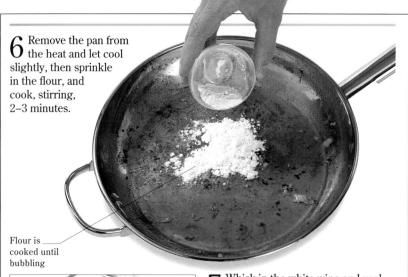

6 Remove the pan from the heat and let cool slightly, then sprinkle in the flour, and cook, stirring, 2–3 minutes.

Flour is cooked until bubbling

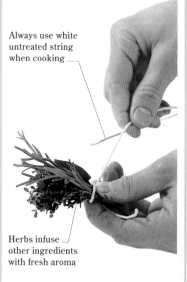

HOW TO MAKE A BOUQUET GARNI

This bundle of aromatic flavouring herbs is designed to be easily lifted from the pan and discarded at the end of cooking. To make a bouquet garni, hold together 2–3 sprigs of fresh thyme, 1 bay leaf, and 5–6 parsley stalks. Wind a piece of white string around the herb stalks and tie them together securely.

Always use white untreated string when cooking

Herbs infuse other ingredients with fresh aroma

7 Whisk in the white wine and veal stock or water. Add the bouquet garni and pepper, and bring to a boil.

ANNE SAYS
"*Whisk constantly when adding the liquid to ensure a smooth sauce results.*"

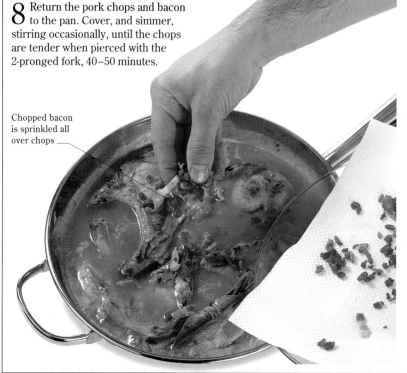

8 Return the pork chops and bacon to the pan. Cover, and simmer, stirring occasionally, until the chops are tender when pierced with the 2-pronged fork, 40–50 minutes.

Chopped bacon is sprinkled all over chops

9 Meanwhile, strip the parsley leaves from the stalks and pile the leaves on the chopping board. With the chef's knife, finely chop them.

2 FINISH THE DISH

1 Transfer the pork chops to a plate and keep warm. Add the cream to the pan and bring just to a boil. Take the pan from the heat.

Double cream mellows and enriches sauce

2 Remove and discard the bouquet garni, and whisk in the mustard. Return the chops to the pan and heat gently so that the flavours blend, 2–3 minutes.

! TAKE CARE !
Do not boil the sauce after adding the mustard or it will be bitter.

🍽 TO SERVE

Arrange the chops, bones pointing upwards, on a warmed platter. Taste the sauce for seasoning, whisking in more mustard if you like. Spoon the sauce over the chops, then sprinkle with the parsley.

Parsley and bacon add bright colour to mustard sauce

V A R I A T I O N

VEAL CHOPS WITH MUSTARD SAUCE AND BABY ONIONS

CÔTES DE VEAU DIJONNAISE AUX PETITS OIGNONS

Veal chops take the place of the pork, while sweet baby onions replace the smoky flavour of the bacon.

1 Omit the pork chops, bacon, and parsley. Prepare 4 veal chops (each weighing about 250 g/8 oz) as for the pork chops. Put 500 g (1 lb) baby onions into a bowl, pour over boiling water to cover, and let stand, 2 minutes. Drain the baby onions, then peel them, leaving a little of the root to hold them together.

2 Heat 15 ml (1 tbsp) vegetable oil in a frying pan, add the baby onions, and cook, stirring, until golden brown, 5–7 minutes. Remove the onions with a slotted spoon. Heat 30 g (1 oz) butter in the pan and brown the veal chops as directed for the pork. Pour in the white wine and veal stock or water, and add the bouquet garni. Cover, then simmer the chops, 20 minutes. Add the onions and continue cooking until the chops and onions are tender, 20–30 minutes longer. Finish the sauce as directed.

COURGETTE TIAN

Tian de Courgettes

EQUIPMENT

1.5 litre (2⅓ pint) baking dish

colander

bowls

saucepan

large frying pan

small knife

chef's knife

slotted spoon

wooden spoon

pastry brush

large plate

chopping board

INGREDIENTS

courgettes

Parmesan cheese

flat-leaf parsley†

olive oil

eggs

long-grain rice

onions

garlic cloves

†curly parsley can also be used

ANNE SAYS
"Be sure to use small courgettes, which tend to have more flavour than large ones."

Tian *is the Provençal name for a shallow earthenware dish used for baking vegetable gratins, such as this mixture of sautéed courgette and onion held together with eggs and cooked rice, which is also known as a* tian. *The flavourings – olive oil, garlic, flat-leaf parsley, and Parmesan cheese – are typical of Provence. This tian is equally delicious served as a first course, or as an accompaniment to dishes of roast lamb or chicken.*

GETTING AHEAD

The tian can be baked up to 1 day ahead and kept, covered, in the refrigerator. Reheat it in a low oven before serving, or serve it at room temperature, if you like.

metric	SHOPPING LIST	imperial
1 kg	courgettes	2 lb
75 ml	olive oil, more for baking dish	2½ fl oz
65 g	long-grain rice	2¼ oz
3	garlic cloves	3
5–7	sprigs of flat-leaf parsley	5–7
2	onions	2
60 g	grated Parmesan cheese	2 oz
3	eggs	3
	salt and pepper	

ORDER OF WORK

1 PREPARE THE INGREDIENTS

2 ASSEMBLE AND BAKE THE TIAN

1 PREPARE THE INGREDIENTS

1 Trim the courgettes, then cut them crossways into 5 mm (1/4 inch) slices with the chef's knife.

2 Heat one-third of the oil in the large frying pan. Add the courgettes and salt and pepper, and cook over medium heat, stirring occasionally, until tender and brown, 10–15 minutes.

3 Transfer the courgettes from the pan to the large plate. Let cool. Meanwhile, cook the rice.

Courgettes should be nicely browned

Spread courgettes over plate to cool

HOW TO SLICE AN ONION

Onions are often sliced for soups and stews, as well as for sautéing. The root end is left on while slicing, to help hold the onion together.

Cut onion into slices of even thickness

1 Using a chef's knife, cut the onion lengthways in half through the root and stalk ends.

2 Lay each half, cut-side down, on a chopping board, and cut across into thin or thick slices, as required.

4 Bring a saucepan of salted water to a boil, add the rice, and bring back to a boil. Simmer until just tender, stirring occasionally, 10–12 minutes.

5 Drain the rice in the colander, rinse with cold water, and drain again thoroughly. Let the rice cool, 8–10 minutes, then stir with a fork to separate the grains.

6 Set the flat side of the chef's knife on top of each garlic clove and strike it with your fist. Discard the skin and finely chop the cloves.

7 Strip the parsley leaves from the stalks and pile the leaves on the chopping board. Using the chef's knife, finely chop them.

8 Peel the onions with the small knife, leaving a little of the root attached. Halve and thinly slice the onions (see box, page 93). Heat half of the remaining oil in the frying pan, add the onions and garlic and cook, stirring occasionally, until soft, 3–5 minutes.

2 ASSEMBLE AND BAKE THE TIAN

2 In a large bowl, combine the chopped courgettes, onion mixture, parsley, rice, and Parmesan cheese. Stir to mix, then taste for seasoning.

Parmesan adds robust flavour

1 Heat the oven to 180°C (350°F, Gas 4). Brush the baking dish with oil. Coarsely chop the cooled courgettes.

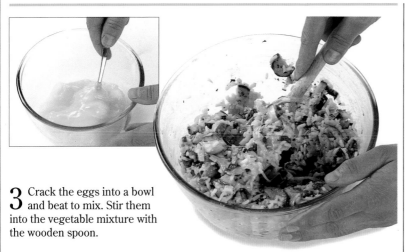

3 Crack the eggs into a bowl and beat to mix. Stir them into the vegetable mixture with the wooden spoon.

4 Spread the mixture in the baking dish and sprinkle with the remaining oil. Bake the tian in the heated oven until set, 10–15 minutes. Increase the oven temperature to 200°C (400°F, Gas 6) and bake until brown, 10–15 minutes longer.

Edges of tian are crisp, while the centre is creamy

¶◎¶ TO SERVE

Serve the tian hot or at room temperature, directly from the baking dish.

Tian is served as accompaniment to roast meats and poultry

VARIATION

SPINACH AND MUSHROOM TIAN

TIAN D'EPINARDS ET CHAMPIGNONS

Spinach and mushrooms are a tasty alternative to courgettes.

1 Omit the courgettes, rice, and parsley. Trim the crusts from 2 slices of white bread. Work the bread slices in a food processor to form fine crumbs. Chop the onions and garlic as directed.
2 Discard the tough ribs and stalks from 1 kg (2 lb) spinach, then wash the leaves. Bring a large saucepan of salted water to a boil. Add the spinach, and simmer until tender, 1–2 minutes. Drain the spinach, rinse with cold water, and drain again. Squeeze the spinach in your fist to remove excess water, then chop coarsely. Wipe 375 g (12 oz) mushrooms, trim the stalks, then thinly slice the caps.
3 Heat 30 ml (2 tbsp) olive oil in a large frying pan and cook the onions and garlic as directed. Add the mushrooms to the pan and sauté until tender, about 5 minutes. Add the spinach and salt and pepper and continue cooking, stirring occasionally, until all the liquid has evaporated, about 5 minutes longer. Let the vegetable mixture cool, then stir in the Parmesan cheese. Taste for seasoning. Prepare a baking dish as directed.
4 Beat the eggs, then stir them into the vegetable mixture. Spoon into the prepared baking dish and sprinkle with the breadcrumbs and 30 ml (2 tbsp) olive oil. Bake as directed.

GRATIN DAUPHINOIS

 SERVES 6–8   WORK TIME 30–40 MINUTES   BAKING TIME 20–25 MINUTES

EQUIPMENT

mandoline†

nutmeg grater

small knife

bowls

vegetable peeler

whisk

pastry brush

colander

wooden spoon

medium saucepan

1.5 litre (2½ pint) shallow baking dish

tea towel   cheese grater

chopping board

†chef's knife can also be used

In this wonderfully rich recipe, the potatoes are first simmered in milk to remove their bitterness, then cooked in double cream, and finally topped with grated Gruyère cheese to brown in the oven. Superb!

— GETTING AHEAD —

The gratin can be assembled up to 1 day ahead and kept, covered, in the refrigerator. Bake it just before serving.

metric	SHOPPING LIST	imperial
750 g	potatoes	1½ lb
600 ml	milk	1 pint
	freshly grated nutmeg	
	salt and pepper	
300 ml	double cream	½ pint
45 g	Gruyère cheese	1½ oz
1	garlic clove	1
	melted butter for baking dish	

INGREDIENTS

potatoes   Gruyère cheese

butter   nutmeg†

garlic clove

double cream

milk

†ground nutmeg can also be used

ANNE SAYS
"Baking potatoes work best for this gratin."

ORDER OF WORK

1 PREPARE THE POTATOES

2 ASSEMBLE AND BAKE THE GRATIN

1 PREPARE THE POTATOES

1 Peel the potatoes. With the mandoline, cut the potatoes crossways into 3 mm (1/8 inch) slices. Alternatively, with the chef's knife, cut a thin slice from one side of each potato so that the potatoes sit flat on the chopping board, and cut them into 3 mm (1/8 inch) slices. Cover the slices with the wet tea towel so that they do not discolour.

! TAKE CARE !
Do not soak the potatoes in water. This removes the starch that will give the gratin its creamy consistency.

Keep fingertips away from blade of mandoline

Potatoes are thinly sliced so they are tender after baking

2 Bring the milk to a boil in the medium saucepan. Season it with a little grated nutmeg, and salt and pepper.

! TAKE CARE !
Stir the milk occasionally with a whisk so that it does not burn.

3 Add the potatoes and cook, stirring occasionally, until the potatoes are just tender, 10–15 minutes.

Freshly grated nutmeg is more aromatic than ground

4 Drain the potatoes in the colander. Discard the milk, or save it for another use such as soup, if you like.

2 ASSEMBLE AND BAKE THE GRATIN

1 Return the potatoes to the saucepan and pour in the cream. Bring to a boil and simmer, stirring occasionally, until the potatoes are very tender, 10–15 minutes. Taste for seasoning.

ANNE SAYS
"After cooking, the cream should be just lightly thickened with starch from the potatoes."

2 Coarsely grate the cheese, and set aside. Heat the oven to 190°C (375°F, Gas 5).

Cream will be simmered gently so it does not evaporate

Potatoes should not break up during cooking

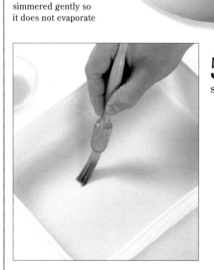

3 Peel the garlic clove, cut it in half, and use the cut side to rub the bottom and sides of the baking dish.

5 Layer the potatoes and cream in the prepared baking dish, then sprinkle with the grated cheese.

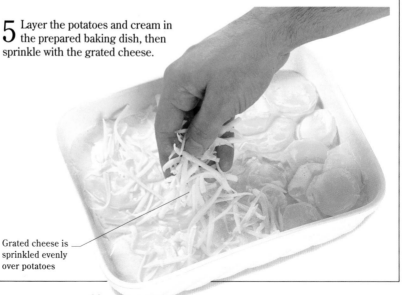

4 Brush the bottom and sides of the baking dish with melted butter, using the pastry brush.

Grated cheese is sprinkled evenly over potatoes

6 Bake the gratin in the heated oven until golden brown, 20–25 minutes. Test with the small knife; the blade should feel hot when withdrawn.

🍴 **TO SERVE**
Serve the Gratin Dauphinois hot, directly from the baking dish.

Gratin Dauphinois is an excellent accompaniment to grilled and roast meats

V A R I A T I O N
GRATIN OF ROOT VEGETABLES
GRATIN DE RACINES D'HIVER

Root vegetables replace half of the potatoes in this version of Gratin Dauphinois. I have chosen carrots, but any root vegetable, such as celeriac or turnips, will do. The carrot slices can be arranged in alternate rows with the potatoes.

1 Peel and trim 375 g (12 oz) carrots. Thinly slice the carrots with a mandoline or chef's knife. Bring 300 ml (1/2 pint) milk to a boil, and season with a little grated nutmeg, and salt and pepper. Add the carrots and simmer until they are almost tender, 15–20 minutes.

2 Meanwhile, peel and slice 375 g (12 oz) potatoes, and simmer them in another 300 ml (1/2 pint) milk as directed. Prepare 6 individual baking dishes as directed for the large baking dish.

3 Drain the carrots and potatoes in a colander. Simmer them together in the cream, and finish the gratin as directed. Serves 6.

Twice-cooked potatoes are meltingly tender

CHERRY CLAFOUTIS

Clafoutis aux Cerises

 SERVES 6–8   WORK TIME 20–25 MINUTES   BAKING TIME 30–35 MINUTES

EQUIPMENT

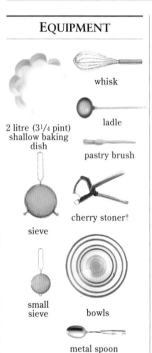

whisk

ladle

pastry brush

2 litre (3¹/₄ pint) shallow baking dish

cherry stoner†

sieve

small sieve

bowls

metal spoon

chopping board

INGREDIENTS

cherries

icing sugar

caster sugar

egg yolks

double cream

plain flour

kirsch

eggs

butter

milk

In this dessert from the Limousin in central France, cherries are baked in an egg batter that puffs up and turns golden. Tart cherries give the most flavour; I like to remove the stones, although this is not traditional. Whipped cream is the best accompaniment.

GETTING AHEAD

The clafoutis is best freshly baked and served warm, but it can also be cooked up to 6 hours ahead and served at room temperature.

ANNE SAYS

"If fresh cherries are not available, you can use two 500 g (1 lb) cans of cherries packed in water."

ORDER OF WORK

1 PREPARE THE CHERRIES AND MAKE THE BATTER

2 ASSEMBLE THE CLAFOUTIS

metric	SHOPPING LIST	imperial
	butter for baking dish	
100 g	caster sugar, more for baking dish	3¹/₂ oz
625 g	cherries	1¹/₄ lb
45 g	plain flour	1¹/₂ oz
	salt	
150 ml	milk	5 fl oz
75 ml	double cream	2¹/₂ fl oz
4	eggs	4
2	egg yolks	2
45 ml	kirsch	3 tbsp
30 ml	icing sugar	2 tbsp

†vegetable peeler can also be used

1 PREPARE THE CHERRIES AND MAKE THE BATTER

1 Brush the baking dish with melted butter. Sprinkle some caster sugar into the dish. Turn the dish around and shake it to coat the bottom and side evenly.

2 Turn the dish upside-down and tap the base with your knuckles to remove any excess sugar.

3 Stone the fresh cherries (see box, below). Alternatively, drain the canned cherries. Spread the cherries in an even layer over the bottom of the prepared baking dish.

4 Sift the flour and a pinch of salt into a medium bowl and make a well in the centre with your fingers.

HOW TO STONE CHERRIES

Choose firm cherries with a shiny skin; avoid any with a dry stalk.

Use tip of vegetable peeler to work stone from cherry

To stone with a cherry stoner: push the stone through the fruit, leaving a hollow. Stoning allows more of the juice to be released when the cherries are cooked.

To stone with a vegetable peeler: insert the tip in the stalk end, rotate around the stone, and scoop it out. The result is neater than if a stoner is used, and more of the juices will be retained.

Eggs and sugar are added to flour mixture at same time

5 Pour the milk and cream into the well and stir with a whisk, gradually drawing in the flour to make a smooth paste.

6 Add the eggs, egg yolks, and caster sugar, and continue whisking to make a smooth batter.

ANNE SAYS
"There is no need to whisk the batter vigorously."

Additional egg yolks add richness to clafoutis

2 ASSEMBLE THE CLAFOUTIS

Batter is easy to pour with ladle

Batter partly covers cherries

1 Heat the oven to 180°C (350°F, Gas 4). Just before baking, ladle the batter over the cherries, then spoon over the kirsch.

2 Bake the clafoutis in the heated oven until puffed up and beginning to brown, 30–35 minutes.

ANNE SAYS
"When cooked, the clafoutis will pull away from the side of the baking dish."

VARIATION

PLUM CLAFOUTIS

CLAFOUTIS AUX PRUNES

Clafoutis with cherries is a dessert of early summer. In autumn and winter, other fresh or dried fruits are used instead, such as any type of small plum.

3 Just before serving, sprinkle the clafoutis with the icing sugar, using the small sieve.

🍴 **TO SERVE**
Serve the clafoutis warm or at room temperature, with whipped cream if you like.

1 Omit the cherries. Prepare the baking dish and make the batter as directed.

2 Cut 625 g (1¼ lb) small plums in half around the stone. Using both hands, give a quick, sharp twist to each half to loosen it from the stone. Scoop out the stone with the tip of a small knife and discard it

3 Arrange the plums, cut-side up, in the bottom of the prepared baking dish. Assemble, bake, and decorate the clafoutis as directed.

Juicy cherries stud sweet rich batter

Icing sugar decorates top of cherry clafoutis

APRICOT AND HAZELNUT ICE CREAM

Glace Auxerroise

 SERVES 6   WORK TIME 35–40 MINUTES*   ❄ FREEZING TIME AT LEAST 4 HOURS**

EQUIPMENT

chef's knife

whisk

food processor†

 ice-cream scoop

sieve

bowls

small knife

 ice-cream maker

tea towel

cling film

small jar with lid

rubber spatula

wooden spoon

 saucepans, 1 heavy-based with lid

† blender can also be used

Vanilla ice cream is transformed by hazelnuts and dried apricots in this Burgundian recipe. A hazelnut liqueur, such as Frangelico, adds sparkle.

GETTING AHEAD

The ice cream can be made up to 2 weeks ahead and kept, tightly covered, in the freezer. If it has been frozen more than 12 hours, let it soften for about 30 minutes in the refrigerator before serving.
plus up to 2 days soaking time
**freezing time varies according to the ice-cream maker you use*

metric	SHOPPING LIST	imperial
90 g	dried apricot halves	3 oz
175 ml	hazelnut liqueur	6 fl oz
125 g	hazelnuts	4 oz
	For the vanilla ice cream	
600 ml	milk	1 pint
1	vanilla pod	1
135 g	caster sugar	4 1/2 oz
8	egg yolks	8
30 ml	cornflour	2 tbsp
250 ml	double cream	8 fl oz

INGREDIENTS

 dried apricot halves

 milk

 caster sugar

 cornflour

vanilla pod†

 hazelnuts

 egg yolks

 double cream

 hazelnut liqueur‡

†1 tsp vanilla essence can also be used

‡apricot brandy can also be used

ORDER OF WORK

1 PREPARE THE APRICOTS AND HAZELNUTS

2 MAKE THE VANILLA CUSTARD

3 FREEZE THE ICE CREAM

1 PREPARE THE APRICOTS AND HAZELNUTS

1 Put the apricots into a bowl and pour over enough boiling water to cover them. Let soak, 10–15 minutes.

2 Drain the apricots and put them into the small jar. Pour over the hazelnut liqueur and cover tightly. Let soak, at least 2 hours, and up to 2 days.

Hazelnut liqueur is reserved to serve with ice cream

Apricots will have more flavour the longer they macerate

3 Strain the apricots, reserving the liqueur. Purée the apricots in a food processor and set aside.

4 Toast and skin the hazelnuts (see box, right). With the chef's knife, coarsely chop the hazelnuts. Reserve half of the nuts for serving.

ANNE SAYS

"*If you are making the ice cream well ahead, store the reserved hazelnuts and liqueur in covered containers.*"

HOW TO TOAST AND SKIN NUTS

Toasting nuts intensifies their flavour and adds crunch to their texture. It also loosens the skin from nuts such as hazelnuts for easy removal.

Hazelnut skins will come off easily after toasting

1 Heat the oven to 180°C (350°F, Gas 4). Toast the nuts on a baking sheet until lightly browned, stirring occasionally, 12–15 minutes.

2 While the nuts are still hot, rub them in a tea towel to remove the skins, then let cool.

2 MAKE THE VANILLA CUSTARD

1 Pour the milk into the heavy-based saucepan. Cut the vanilla pod lengthways, if using. Add to the pan. Bring the milk just to a boil. Remove from the heat. Cover, and let stand in a warm place, 10–15 minutes.

2 Set aside one-quarter of the milk. Add the sugar to the remaining hot milk and stir with the wooden spoon until dissolved.

3 Beat the egg yolks with the cornflour in a medium bowl. Add the sweetened hot milk and whisk just until the mixture is smooth.

4 Pour the custard back into the saucepan and cook over medium heat, stirring constantly with the wooden spoon, until it comes just to a boil and thickens enough to coat the back of the spoon. Your finger will leave a clear trail across the spoon.

5 Remove the pan from the heat, stir in the reserved milk, then strain the custard into a bowl. Stir in the vanilla essence, if using. Cover tightly with cling film to prevent a skin forming on the surface of the custard and let cool.

ANNE SAYS
"*The vanilla pod can be rinsed and dried to use again.*"

Custard is strained to remove vanilla pod and any bits of cooked egg yolk

3 FREEZE THE ICE CREAM

1 If the vanilla custard has formed a skin, whisk to dissolve it. Pour the custard into the ice-cream maker and freeze until slushy, following the manufacturer's directions. Meanwhile, chill 2 medium bowls in the freezer.

2 Pour the cream into one of the chilled bowls and whip until soft peaks form.

ANNE SAYS
"*Cream thickens faster when whipped in a chilled bowl.*"

Use rubber
spatula to stir
ice cream

3 Add half of the
hazelnuts and the
apricot purée to the
slushy vanilla ice
cream and stir
until mixed.

Hazelnuts give
crunchy finish to
ice cream

4 Add the whipped cream, stir
lightly, and continue freezing in
the ice-cream maker until firm.
Transfer the ice cream to the second
chilled bowl. Cover tightly and store
in the freezer.

🍴 **TO SERVE**
Scoop the ice cream into chilled
individual glasses, spoon over the
reserved hazelnut liqueur, top
with the reserved hazelnuts,
and serve at once.

Tall sundae glasses
are ideal for serving
ice cream

VARIATION

PRUNE AND ARMAGNAC ICE CREAM

GLACE GASCONNE

*A combination of two Gascon
favourites, prunes and
Armagnac, flavours this ice
cream – a fine end to any
festive meal.*

1 Omit the apricots, hazelnut liqueur,
and hazelnuts. Put 150 g
(5 oz) pitted prunes into a
small bowl. Pour over
175 ml (6 fl oz)
Armagnac and let
the prunes soak as
directed for the
apricots. Strain the
prunes, reserving the liqueur.
Purée the prunes.

2 Make and chill the vanilla
custard as directed. Make
and freeze the ice cream as
directed, substituting the
prunes and Armagnac for
the apricots and hazelnut
liqueur. Serve the ice
cream with the reserved
liqueur as directed, topped
with more pitted prunes, if
you like.

GOLDEN RICE PUDDING WITH PEACHES AND RED WINE

Terrinée et Chicolle

 SERVES 4–6 WORK TIME 15–20 MINUTES* COOKING TIME 4 HOURS

EQUIPMENT

chef's knife

slotted spoon

1.5 litre
(2¹/₃ pint)
ovenproof
bowl

wooden spoon

large
metal spoon

saucepan   metal spoon

small knife

bowls,   paper towels
1 non-metallic

chopping board

INGREDIENTS

peaches

short-grain
rice

milk

dry red
wine

caster sugar

cinnamon
stick

ANNE SAYS
"*Short-grain rice contains
more starch than long or
medium-grain rice and
absorbs more milk, making
the pudding richer.*"

*The long cooking for this rice pudding results
in a creamy dessert hidden beneath a sweet
golden crust. In summer, I like to serve it just
warm, accompanied by chilled peaches
macerated in red wine.*

GETTING AHEAD
Both the rice pudding and peaches can be prepared
1 day ahead and kept, covered, in the refrigerator. Let the
rice come to room temperature, or warm it in a low oven
before serving.
*plus at least 2 hours macerating and 1 hour standing time

metric	SHOPPING LIST	imperial
65 g	short-grain rice	2¹/₄ oz
1 litre	milk, more if needed	1²/₃ pints
1	5 cm (2 inch) piece of cinnamon stick	1
50 g	caster sugar	1³/₄ oz
	salt	
	For the chicolle	
4	ripe peaches	4
60 g	caster sugar, more if needed	2 oz
250 ml	dry red wine, more if needed	8 fl oz

ORDER OF WORK

1 MACERATE THE
PEACHES IN RED
WINE

2 MAKE THE RICE
PUDDING

1 MACERATE THE PEACHES IN RED WINE

Blanched peaches retain their shape

Peaches are cooled in cold water so they do not cook

1 Peel and stone the peaches: bring a saucepan of water to a boil. Immerse the peaches in the water, 10 seconds, then transfer them to a bowl of cold water.

ANNE SAYS
"If the peaches are very ripe, you may not need to put them into boiling water before peeling."

2 Using the small knife, cut each peach in half, using the indentation on one side as a guide.

3 With both hands, give a sharp twist to each peach half to loosen it from the stone. If the peaches cling, loosen the flesh with the chef's knife.

5 Carefully peel the skin from each of the peach halves and discard it.

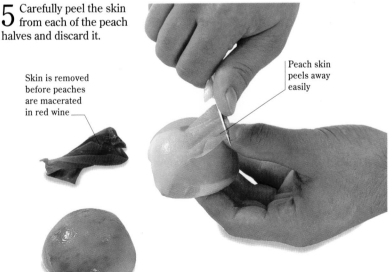

Skin is removed before peaches are macerated in red wine

Peach skin peels away easily

4 Lift or scoop out each stone from the centre of its peach half and discard it.

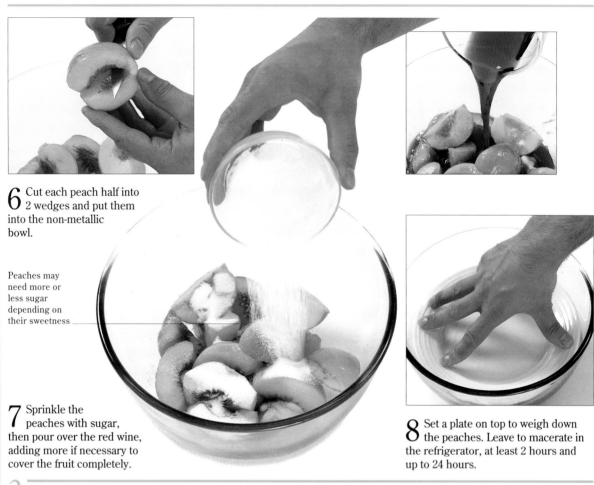

6 Cut each peach half into 2 wedges and put them into the non-metallic bowl.

Peaches may need more or less sugar depending on their sweetness

7 Sprinkle the peaches with sugar, then pour over the red wine, adding more if necessary to cover the fruit completely.

8 Set a plate on top to weigh down the peaches. Leave to macerate in the refrigerator, at least 2 hours and up to 24 hours.

2 MAKE THE RICE PUDDING

2 Wipe the side of the bowl clean with a damp paper towel. Transfer the bowl to the heated oven and bake. Stir the mixture gently every 30 minutes by slipping the metal spoon down the side of the bowl and stirring from the bottom, until a golden crust forms, 4 hours. The pudding will be soupy throughout cooking.

! TAKE CARE !
At the end of cooking, a golden crust will form. Try not to break the crust.

1 Heat the oven to 150°C (300°F, Gas 2). In the ovenproof bowl, combine the rice, milk, cinnamon stick, sugar, and a pinch of salt. Stir with the wooden spoon until well mixed.

Cinnamon stick flavours rice pudding during long baking

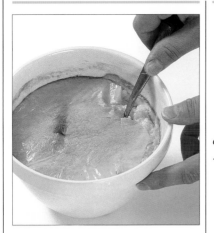

3 Remove the pudding from the oven. Carefully slip the spoon down the side of the bowl, and stir the mixture from the bottom. Let the pudding stand to completely absorb the milk, 1 hour.

ANNE SAYS
"The pudding will be soupy until it cools."

¡©¡ TO SERVE
Remove and discard the cinnamon stick from the rice pudding. Divide the pudding among individual bowls, then spoon over the peaches with some of the red wine syrup.

VARIATION

RICE PUDDING WITH DRIED FRUIT COMPOTE

TERRINEE AU CONFIT DE FRUITS SECS

A quickly cooked compote of dried fruit – half fruit salad, half preserve – adds a contrast of texture and flavour to creamy rice pudding.

1 Omit the peaches, 60 g (2 oz) sugar, and the red wine. Prepare the rice pudding as directed. Meanwhile, prepare the dried fruit compote.
2 Cut 100 g (3½ oz) dried figs into eighths and 100 g (3½ oz) dried apricot halves across into 4 slices each. With a vegetable peeler, peel the zest from 1 lemon half.
3 Put the lemon zest into a small saucepan with 90 g (3 oz) sugar and 1 whole clove. Add 175 ml (6 fl oz) water and heat, stirring occasionally, until the sugar dissolves. Bring to a boil, add the figs, and simmer until softened, about 5 minutes.
4 Add the apricots and 30 ml (2 tbsp) sultanas and continue simmering until the fruit is puffed up and tender, about 5 minutes more.
5 Remove the pan from the heat, stir in 30 ml (2 tbsp) brandy, and let stand until all of the liquid is absorbed, 5–10 minutes. Remove and discard the whole clove. Serve the compote warm or hot with the rice pudding.

Red wine syrup is refreshing accompaniment to creamy rice pudding

Peach wedges are richly flavoured with wine

SNOW EGGS

Oeufs à la Neige

 SERVES 8 WORK TIME 35–40 MINUTES COOKING TIME 45–50 MINUTES

EQUIPMENT

slotted spoon

wooden spoon

whisk

small frying pan

small knife

large metal bowl   paper towels

rubber spatula

bowls

medium heavy-based saucepan with lid

large wide pan   sieve

dessert spoons

cling film

baking sheet

In this time-honoured French dessert, egg whites are whipped into a simple meringue, then moulded into egg shapes and poached in water. The meringues are served on a pool of vanilla custard sauce and decorated with flaked almonds and trails of caramel.

GETTING AHEAD

The vanilla custard sauce can be prepared up to 1 day ahead and kept, covered, in the refrigerator. Poach the snow eggs not more than 6 hours before serving; keep them, tightly covered, in the refrigerator. Make the caramel and finish the dessert just before serving.

metric	SHOPPING LIST	imperial
	For the vanilla custard sauce	
750 ml	milk	1¼ pints
1	vanilla pod	1
100 g	caster sugar	3½ oz
8	egg yolks	8
30 ml	cornflour	2 tbsp
	For the meringue eggs	
8	egg whites	8
	salt	
400 g	caster sugar	14 oz
	For the decoration	
45 g	flaked almonds	1½ oz
200 g	caster sugar	6½ oz
125 ml	water	4 fl oz

INGREDIENTS

caster sugar

flaked almonds

vanilla pod†

milk

egg yolks

egg whites

cornflour

† 1 tsp vanilla essence can also be used

ORDER OF WORK

1 MAKE THE VANILLA CUSTARD SAUCE AND TOAST THE ALMONDS

2 MAKE AND POACH THE MERINGUE EGGS

3 MAKE THE CARAMEL AND FINISH THE DISH

1 MAKE THE VANILLA CUSTARD SAUCE AND TOAST THE ALMONDS

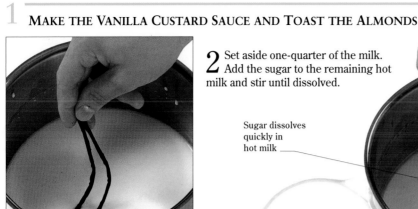

2 Set aside one-quarter of the milk. Add the sugar to the remaining hot milk and stir until dissolved.

Sugar dissolves quickly in hot milk

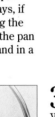

1 Pour the milk into the saucepan. Cut the vanilla pod lengthways, if using, and add to the milk. Bring the milk just to a boil, then remove the pan from the heat. Cover, and let stand in a warm place, 10–15 minutes.

3 Beat the egg yolks with the cornflour in a medium bowl. Whisk in the sweetened hot milk just until the mixture is smooth.

4 Pour the custard back into the saucepan and cook over medium heat, stirring constantly, until it comes just to a boil and is thick enough to coat the back of the spoon; the custard will curdle if boiled further.

Finger leaves clear trail across spoon

5 Remove the pan from the heat, stir in the reserved milk, then strain the custard into a bowl. Rinse the vanilla pod, dry, and store to use again. Stir in the vanilla essence, if using. Cover tightly with cling film to prevent a skin from forming on the surface of the custard, and let cool. Finally, chill the custard sauce.

Reserved milk adjusts consistency of custard

6 Heat the oven to 180°C (350°F, Gas 4). Spread the almonds on the baking sheet and toast in the oven until lightly browned, stirring occasionally so that they colour evenly, 10–12 minutes. Set the almonds aside.

2 MAKE AND POACH THE MERINGUE EGGS

Sugar is added while egg whites are whisked

Egg whites are shaped into neat ovals

1 Put the egg whites into the metal bowl with a pinch of salt and whisk until stiff. Sprinkle in 60–75 g (2–2½ oz) of the sugar, and continue whisking until glossy to make a light meringue, about 30 seconds.

2 Using the rubber spatula, fold the remaining sugar into the meringue mixture gradually and thoroughly, 1–2 minutes, or until the meringue forms long peaks when the spatula is lifted from the bowl.

3 Bring a large wide pan of water to a simmer. Dip a dessert spoon into the water, and scoop out a large spoonful of meringue. Use a second spoon to shape the meringue into a neat oval, turning the spoons one against the other.

5 Lift the meringue eggs out of the water with the slotted spoon and drain on paper towels. Shape and cook the remaining meringue in the same way.

ANNE SAYS
"The meringue eggs will deflate slightly as they cool."

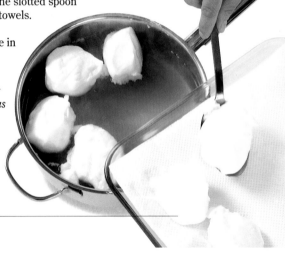

4 Drop the meringue egg into the simmering water. Quickly continue shaping 6–7 more eggs, dipping the spoons into the water so that they do not stick. Poach the eggs until firm and puffed, 5–7 minutes.

Meringues are drained on paper towels to remove excess water

3 MAKE THE CARAMEL AND FINISH THE DISH

1 Pour the chilled custard sauce into a wide shallow serving dish. Using the slotted spoon, arrange the meringue eggs over the custard.

2 Make the caramel: put the sugar and water into a small frying pan and heat gently until the sugar is dissolved, stirring occasionally. Bring the sugar syrup to a boil, and boil without stirring until the syrup starts to turn golden around the edge, 8–10 minutes.

3 Lower the heat and continue cooking until the caramel is a deep golden brown, swirling it in the pan once or twice so that it colours evenly. Remove the pan from the heat and immediately plunge the base into a bowl of cold water to stop the caramel cooking.

! TAKE CARE !
Do not overcook the caramel because it burns easily.

4 Dry the base of the pan, then delicately drizzle the caramel over the meringue eggs in a freeform pattern. Alternatively, drizzle the caramel with a spoon.

🍴 **TO SERVE**
Sprinkle the snow eggs with the toasted almonds and serve immediately.

Toasted almonds make a crunchy contrast to light snow eggs and creamy sauce

Caramel gives attractive finish

V A R I A T I O N
CHOCOLATE SNOW EGGS
OEUFS A LA NEIGE AU CHOCOLAT
Here, a chocolate custard sauce accompanies the meringue eggs, which are topped with trails of melted chocolate.

1 Omit the caramel, flaked almonds, and vanilla pod or vanilla essence. Cut 300 g (10 oz) plain chocolate into large chunks. Chop them with a chef's knife, or in a food processor using the pulse button.

2 Make the custard sauce using two-thirds of the chopped chocolate instead of the vanilla pod or vanilla essence. Heat the milk gently, stirring, until melted and smooth. Do not let the milk come to a boil. Continue making the custard sauce as directed.

3 Make and poach 18 meringue eggs as directed. Heat the reserved chopped chocolate in a bowl set in a saucepan of hot water, stirring occasionally, until just melted.

4 Spoon the chocolate custard into 6 shallow individual bowls and divide the snow eggs among them. With a spoon, drizzle the melted chocolate over the snow eggs. Serves 6.

RUSTIC APPLE TART

Tarte aux Pommes Ménagère

 SERVES 6–8   WORK TIME 40–45 MINUTES*   BAKING TIME 30–40 MINUTES

EQUIPMENT

chef's knife

thin-bladed knife

25 cm (10 inch) flan tin with removable base

melon baller

pastry brush

small knife

bowls

vegetable peeler

cling film

sieve

rolling pin

baking sheet

frying pan

rubber spatula

wooden spoon

wire rack

small saucepan

pastry scraper

chopping board

Every French housewife has her own version of tarte aux pommes. *This recipe comes from Normandy and is the pride of our friend Françoise Samson, whose cooking delighted us when we lived just down the road.*

GETTING AHEAD

The pâte sucrée dough can be made up to 2 days ahead and kept, tightly wrapped, in the refrigerator. The apple tart is best freshly baked.

*plus 45 minutes chilling time

INGREDIENTS

cooking apples

 vanilla essence

salt   caster sugar

butter   plain flour

apricot jam

lemon juice

egg yolks

metric	SHOPPING LIST	imperial
1.4 kg	cooking apples	3 lb
30 g	butter	1 oz
5 ml	vanilla essence	1 tsp
60 g	caster sugar, more to taste	2 oz
	juice of 1/2 lemon	
	For the pâte sucrée dough	
175 g	plain flour, more if needed	6 oz
90 g	unsalted butter, more for flan tin	3 oz
60 g	caster sugar	2 oz
2.5 ml	vanilla essence	1/2 tsp
1.25 ml	salt	1/4 tsp
3	egg yolks	3
	For the glaze	
60 ml	apricot jam	4 tbsp
15–30 ml	water	1–2 tbsp

ORDER OF WORK

1 MAKE THE PATE SUCREE DOUGH AND PREPARE THE APPLES

2 LINE THE FLAN TIN

3 ASSEMBLE AND BAKE THE TART

1 MAKE THE PATE SUCREE DOUGH AND PREPARE THE APPLES

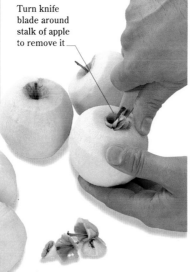

Turn knife blade around stalk of apple to remove it

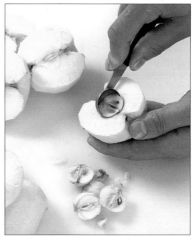

1 Make and chill the pâte sucrée dough (see box, page 118). Make the apple compote: using the vegetable peeler, peel two-thirds of the apples. Cut out the flower and stalk ends of the apples with the small knife.

2 Using the chef's knife, cut each apple in half, then scoop out the cores with the melon baller.

3 Set 1 apple half flat-side down and cut it crossways into 5 mm (¼ inch) slices. Stack the slices and cut them into 5 mm (¼ inch) strips.

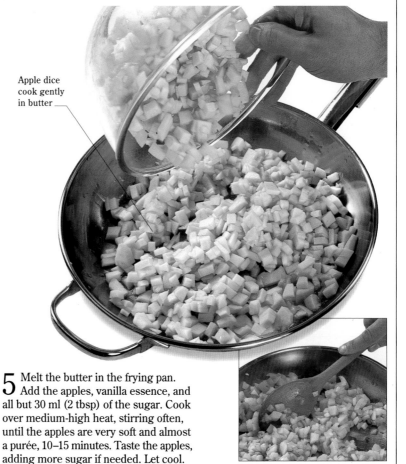

Apple dice cook gently in butter

4 Gather the strips together into a pile and cut crossways into dice. Repeat with the remaining apples.

5 Melt the butter in the frying pan. Add the apples, vanilla essence, and all but 30 ml (2 tbsp) of the sugar. Cook over medium-high heat, stirring often, until the apples are very soft and almost a purée, 10–15 minutes. Taste the apples, adding more sugar if needed. Let cool.

HOW TO MAKE PATE SUCREE DOUGH

The favourite French sweet pastry is pâte sucrée. The high proportion of sugar and eggs yolks gives the dough a crumbly character.

1 Sift the flour onto the work surface and make a well in the centre. Pound the butter with a rolling pin to soften it.

2 Put the sugar, softened butter, vanilla essence, salt, and egg yolks into the well.

Well in flour is large enough for ingredients to be mixed easily

3 With your fingertips, work the ingredients in the well until thoroughly mixed.

4 Draw in the flour with the pastry scraper, then work the flour into the other ingredients with your fingers until coarse crumbs form.

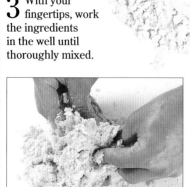

5 With your fingers, press the crumbs firmly together to form a ball of dough. If the dough is sticky, work in a little more flour. Lightly flour the work surface.

6 Blend the dough by pushing it away from you with the heel of your hand, then gathering it up, until it is very smooth and peels away from the work surface, 1–2 minutes.

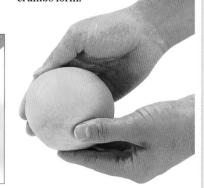

7 Shape the dough into a ball, wrap it tightly in cling film, and chill until firm, about 30 minutes.

Apples are cut into thin slices to arrange in attractive pattern on tart

Lemon juice prevents apple slices from discolouring

6 Peel and core the remaining apples. Set each apple half, flat-side down, on the chopping board. With the thin-bladed knife, cut the apple halves crossways into thin slices.

7 Transfer the apple slices to a medium bowl, sprinkle with the lemon juice, and toss to coat completely.

2 LINE THE FLAN TIN

1 Brush the flan tin with melted butter. Lightly flour the work surface and roll out the chilled dough into a 30 cm (12 inch) round.

2 Wrap the dough around the rolling pin, then unroll it to drape it over the tin. Gently lift the edge of the dough with one hand and press it well into the bottom of the tin with the other hand, pressing to seal any cracks. Overlap the dough slightly inside the rim of the tin so that extra dough is left at the edge of the shell.

Excess dough will be cut away with rolling pin

Rolling pin gives clean edge to dough

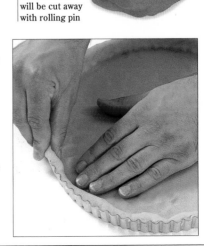

3 Roll the rolling pin over the top of the tin, pressing down to cut off the excess dough.

4 Press the dough evenly up the side, from the bottom, to increase the height of the shell. Chill until firm, about 15 minutes. Heat the oven to 200°C (400°F, Gas 6). Heat the baking sheet in the oven.

ANNE SAYS
"A deep shell leaves plenty of room for filling."

3 ASSEMBLE AND BAKE THE TART

Apple slices are arranged from outside edge to centre of tart

1 Spoon the cooled apple compote over the bottom of the pastry shell. Arrange the apple slices over the compote in overlapping concentric circles. Sprinkle with the remaining sugar.

2 Bake the tart on the baking sheet in the heated oven, until the rim of the pastry begins to turn golden, 15–20 minutes. Lower the oven temperature to 180°C (350°F, Gas 4) and continue baking the tart until the apple slices are tender and the rim of the pastry is golden brown, 15–20 minutes longer. Let the tart cool slightly on the wire rack, then set the flan tin on a bowl to loosen and remove the side.

ANNE SAYS
" The edges of the apple slices should brown to form an attractive pattern. If necessary, grill the tart 2–3 minutes to brown it."

Use rubber spatula to press apricot glaze through sieve

Glaze is sieved to ensure that it is smooth

3 Let the tart cool a little longer, then slide it from the tin base onto a serving platter.

! TAKE CARE !
Do not remove the tin base too soon or the pastry may crack.

4 Meanwhile, make the glaze: in a small saucepan, heat the apricot jam with the water, stirring until melted. Work the jam glaze through a sieve. Return the glaze to the pan and melt again over low heat.

5 Brush the apples and the pastry rim with the apricot glaze.

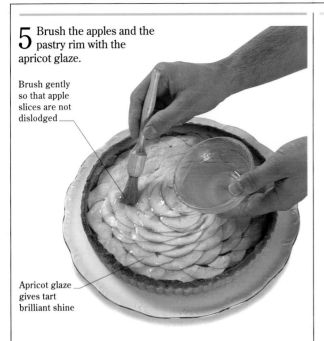

Brush gently so that apple slices are not dislodged

Apricot glaze gives tart brilliant shine

🍽 TO SERVE

Serve warm or at room temperature with crème fraîche or vanilla ice cream, if you like.

Layer of sliced apples conceals filling of sweet apple compote

APPLE TARTLETS

TARTELETTES AUX POMMES

When baked in tartlet moulds, family-style apple tart becomes an elegant dessert. This recipe makes 6 tartlets.

1 Make the pâte sucrée dough and prepare the apples as directed in the main recipe.

2 Brush six 10 cm (4 inch) tartlet moulds with melted butter. Lightly flour the work surface and roll out the chilled dough to a 3 mm (1/8 inch) thickness. Group the tartlet moulds together, with their edges nearly touching. Drape the dough over the moulds and line them as directed. With your fingers, press the dough well into the bottom of each mould and against the side to form a neat shell. Chill until firm, about 15 minutes.

3 Heat the oven to 200°C (400°F, Gas 6). Put a baking sheet in the oven to heat. Spread a few spoonfuls of apple compote over the bottom of each tartlet shell. Arrange the apple slices overlapping on top, then sprinkle them with sugar. Bake the tartlets on the baking sheet in the heated oven until the rim of the pastry and the apples begin to turn golden, about 20 minutes. If you like, grill the apple tartlets as directed. Leave the tartlets to cool as directed, then carefully unmould them.

4 Make the apricot glaze and glaze the tartlets as directed.

FRENCH KNOW-HOW

The French countryside offers an abundance of fresh produce, fine cheeses, and a wide range of meats and poultry. Using a few basic techniques and a handful of traditional recipes, the cook is able to transform these ingredients into the refined yet simple dishes that are handed down from generation to generation.

EQUIPMENT

You won't find much specialized equipment in a French country kitchen because cooks rely on traditional tools. The first essential is a sharp chef's knife for chopping or cutting up meat and poultry, plus one or two smaller knives for vegetables. Keep them sharpened regularly with a steel or stone, and store them carefully so that the blades are not damaged. A whisk is often called for, to blend sauces to silky smoothness, or to whisk a batter or egg whites. Other standard kitchen equipment includes a vegetable peeler, a grater, and a lemon squeezer, as well as wooden spoons for stirring and slotted spoons for lifting foods from liquid or fat. You will also need a sieve, a colander, and a rubber spatula.

There are a few tarts and quiches in this book, calling for a rolling pin and a heavy baking sheet that does not warp, as well as a flan tin, either fluted or plain, with a removable base. It is not advisable to change the size of the tin called for in any of these recipes because the proportions of pastry and filling will be wrong.

The Country Terrine is baked in a long, straight-sided terrine mould with a lid. For crêpes, a small frying pan works well if you don't have a traditional crêpe pan. A large sauté pan or a frying pan, as well as a roasting tin, will also come in handy for many dishes. A shallow, oval or rectangular baking dish is much used in France for baking and browning gratins and stuffed crêpes. I like to choose an attractive dish that can be transferred from oven to table so that food can be served piping hot. Flameproof enamelled cast iron, or plain white heatproof ceramic dishes are particularly popular. Choose a dish that has low sides so that the oven heat dries the topping and turns it a crispy golden brown. For braising chicken and rabbit or making a lamb stew, a large, heavy casserole with a tight-fitting lid and heatproof handles is essential – be sure the base is thick enough to prevent scorching during the slow cooking. It is important to remember that a pots and pans should fit their purpose.

You won't find a food processor in a traditional French kitchen, but, for some of the recipes in this book, it will save time in chopping and puréeing. A blender can be used instead, but the ingredients may need to be worked in batches. An electric mixer takes all the hard work out of whisking cream and egg whites.

INGREDIENTS

Even the smallest French country town boasts a weekly open market. On a market day townspeople rise early to search for locally grown ingredients – a basket overflowing with fresh produce is on the arm of virtually every pedestrian. Because fresh ingredients are so accessible and of such high quality, meals are organized around what is seasonally available.

France is surrounded on three sides by sea, so it is hardly surprising that, from Brittany in the northwest to sunny Provence in the south, seafood is the focus of many menus. The recipes in this book for prawns, scallops, sole, and sea bass are just a beginning. Poultry is often the focus of the midday meal. Here you'll find several ideas for chicken to be sautéed, or marinated and then simmered in a sauce, with more recipes for duck and poussin. The four main meats, particularly pork, are also common choices, often simmered until tender with vegetables, wine, and stock in a rich stew.

Vegetables do not just act as accompaniments in French cooking, they play a vital role in flavouring all manner of dishes. Most important is the allium family – onion, garlic, leeks, and shallots. Carrots and celery are a close second, with tomatoes, mushrooms, potatoes, and other roots as common additions. The south revels in vine-ripened tomatoes, peppers, aubergines, and courgettes, while in Burgundy wild mushrooms are so common in the autumn that it is not unusual to see whole families combing the woods for the precious fungi.

Depending on the season, you may find fruit paired with savoury dishes as a foil to a piquant sauce. In autumn, duck is often matched with pears, while earlier in the year the choice may be fresh cherries. Fresh fruit is also a favourite ending to a meal, particularly in summer. In winter, dried and fresh fruits such as apples frequently appear as desserts, baked into tarts and cakes. Dairy products are a mainstay of the French kitchen, with butter adding characteristic flavour to sauces such as *beurre blanc*, or binding flour in a flaky pastry shell. Stiff, nutty-flavoured crème fraîche is frequently stirred into a savoury sauce, with whipped sweetened Chantilly cream an essential component in many desserts. However, flavoured oils should not be overlooked. In a broad belt running along the Mediterranean, olive oil is the cooking fat of choice, while walnut, hazelnut and other nut oils are favoured inland. In southwestern France, you'll come across goose fat in dessert pastries as well as in savoury dishes.

Parsley, thyme, rosemary, tarragon, and chervil are the common herbs in a French kitchen, often growing freely in the back garden. The fragrant leaves may be stirred into a recipe at the last minute to release fresh flavour and colour, or added at the beginning of cooking so as to blend and marry with other ingredients. Perhaps the most basic ingredient of all is stock, often called the foundation of French cooking. Beef, veal, or chicken stock may be added after roasting to deglaze a pan to make gravy, or to provide the basis for a soup, sauce, or stew.

BEEF OR VEAL STOCK

🍽️ MAKES 2–3 LITRES (3 1/4– 4 2/3 PINTS)

🥄 WORK TIME 20–30 MINUTES

🍲 COOKING TIME 4–5 HOURS

metric	SHOPPING LIST	imperial
2 kg	beef or veal bones, cut into pieces	4 1/2 lb
2	onions, peeled and quartered	2
2	carrots, peeled and quartered	2
2	celery stalks, quartered	2
1	large bouquet garni	1
10	black peppercorns	10
15 ml	tomato purée	1 tbsp

1 Heat the oven to 230°C (450°F, Gas 8). Roast the bones until well browned, stirring often, 30–40 minutes. Add the vegetables and brown, 15–20 minutes.

2 Transfer the bones and vegetables to a stockpot. Discard the fat from the tin, pour in 500 ml (16 fl oz) water, and bring to a boil, stirring. Add to the pot with the remaining ingredients and 3 litres (4 2/3 pints) water. Simmer, uncovered, skimming occasionally and adding water, if needed, 4–5 hours. Strain, and reduce, if you like. Cool, discard the fat, and refrigerate.

FISH STOCK

🍽️ MAKES ABOUT 1 LITRE (1 2/3 PINTS)

🥄 WORK TIME 10–15 MINUTES

🍲 COOKING TIME 20 MINUTES

metric	SHOPPING LIST	imperial
500 g	bones and heads of lean white fish, cut into 5 cm (2 inch) pieces	1 lb
1	onion, thinly sliced	1
250 ml	dry white wine	8 fl oz
3–5	sprigs of parsley	3–5
5 ml	peppercorns	1 tsp

1 Wash the fish bones and heads; place them in a medium saucepan with the remaining ingredients.

2 Pour in 1 litre (1 2/3 pints) water and bring to a boil. Simmer, skimming occasionally with a large metal spoon, 20 minutes.

3 Strain the stock into a bowl. Cool, then cover, and keep in the refrigerator.

CHICKEN STOCK

🍽️ MAKES ABOUT 2 LITRES (3 1/4 PINTS)

🥄 WORK TIME 15 MINUTES

🍲 COOKING TIME UP TO 3 HOURS

metric	SHOPPING LIST	imperial
1–1.15 kg	chicken backs and necks	2–2 1/2 lb
1	onion, quartered	1
1	carrot, quartered	1
1	celery stalk, quartered	1
1	bouquet garni	1
5	peppercorns	5

1 Put the chicken pieces into a large saucepan with the remaining ingredients.

2 Pour in 2 litres (3 1/4 pints) water and bring to a boil. Simmer up to 3 hours, skimming occasionally with a large metal spoon, and adding more water if needed.

3 Strain the stock into a large bowl. Cool, then cover, and keep in the refrigerator.

TECHNIQUES

The French start with good ingredients, then treat them with care in the kitchen. Particular attention is paid to basic techniques, like slicing a vegetable correctly, or simmering a soup at just the right speed. Throughout this book, there are illustrations of basic processes, such as browning poultry, pork, or lamb to enhance their flavour, making a roux by cooking butter with flour to thicken a sauce, and sautéing a wide range of ingredients from mushrooms to chicken. Several of the recipes use less common ingredients, such as rabbit and duck, and you'll see how to prepare them, too.

Cooking methods in this book are equally varied, ranging from roasting meat in Leg of Lamb with Roasted Garlic and Shallots and pan-frying steak in Steak au Poivre to preparing and cooking a whole fish in Roast Sea Bass with Herb Butter Sauce. Braising, simmering, and deep-frying are still more techniques with which you will become familiar. You will learn how to make and bake sweet and savoury pastry doughs, how to fry crêpes, and how to whisk egg whites to poach them into light meringues. Turning to sauces, you will find out how to combine egg yolks, sugar, and milk to make vanilla custard sauce – also the base for ice cream. Preparing a simple cream sauce, or the more delicate *beurre blanc* or butter sauce, is made easy.

As with other volumes in the *Look & Cook* series, basic techniques that are commonly used in the recipes are described in detail. You will see how to chop herbs; how to peel, seed, and chop tomatoes; how to chop and slice onions; how to core and seed peppers and cut them into strips; how to make chicken, beef, veal, and fish stock, how to make a bouquet garni, and how to chop garlic.

MICROWAVE

To speed preparation, some of these recipes can be adapted for microwave cooking, especially when simmering or roasting is involved. For instance, to shorten the simmering time for Spring Lamb Stew, brown the cubes of lamb on top of the stove, then finish cooking the dish in the microwave. Marinate and brown the rabbit as directed for Rabbit with Provençal Herbs and Baked Tomatoes, then finish cooking the rabbit in the microwave. The microwave speeds the lengthy cooking time for Golden Rice Pudding: prepare the ingredients as directed and cook the rice pudding in the microwave. Keep careful watch, however, stirring often for even cooking.

Vegetables cook quickly and easily in the microwave, and because many of these recipes are based on, or filled with, vegetables, it proves a useful tool. For example, cook the spinach and mushrooms for Spinach and Mushroom Gratin in the microwave, transfer them to a baking dish, add the remaining ingredients, and brown in a conventional oven. The red pepper, chilli, and onion garnish for Omelette with Peppers and Tomatoes cooks in minutes in a microwave. Stir it into the egg mixture and finish the omelette on top of the stove. Cook the leeks for the Leek and Cheese Quiche in the microwave, set them in the tart shell with the custard and cheese, and bake in a conventional oven.

The microwave is also helpful in preparing certain basic ingredients. For example, it can ease the peeling of small onions or shallots. Trim 90 g (3 oz) small onions or shallots, put them into a microwave-safe bowl and heat on High (100% power), 45 seconds, then squeeze each stalk end until the onions or shallots pop out of the skins. You can also cook bacon and melt chocolate in the microwave. For all recipes, be sure to follow manufacturers' instructions for cooking speeds and times.

CHEESE IN FRENCH COUNTRY COOKING

Cheese, notably Gruyère and Parmesan, has its place in French cooking, but by far the most cheese is eaten at the table as a separate course. It may appear before dessert, or be paired with fruit and replace dessert altogether.

A platter of cheeses should be a well-balanced contrast of appearance, taste, and texture. I usually choose one hard cheese such as Gruyère or Comté, one blue – bleu d'Auvergne is my favourite, but Roquefort is more common – and one soft, perhaps a wedge of Brie or Pont l'Evêque. There's a huge choice. A round or log of goat cheese is also a common addition. Just to remind you, France is said to have 365 cheeses, one for every day of the year.

Ripeness is most important when selecting cheese, and both odour and appearance are good tests. Hard, aged cheeses should smell nutty, almost spicy, as you hope they will taste, while softer, high-fat cheeses should be aromatic and some even quite pungent. No cheese, however, should be so overripe that it smells of ammonia. Look at the rind of the cheese as well. On hard and blue cheeses the rind should be firm and crusty, but with soft cheese this may indicate that it has been kept too long.

When serving a cheese course, arrange the wedges or rounds on a wooden board or a large, flat decorative plate. Best of all is a flat basket tray lined with edible leaves, such as vine leaves, or with paper napkins or doilies. The cheeses should all be at room temperature, accompanied by the bread of your choice. Nut or raisin breads are particularly good. When slicing the cheese, be sure to cut through the rind so each diner is served a piece of the rind as well as the desirable soft interior.

FRENCH COUNTRY COOKING AND YOUR HEALTH

Regardless of the style of cooking, variety and moderation are the key to a sensible diet. Variety in **French Country Cooking** is easy to achieve, given the wide range of ingredients traditionally used. Be sure to follow the French example of cooking with only the freshest and best-quality products.

If fat and calories are a concern, look to recipes where little fat is used in the cooking process, such as roasting, simmering, and sautéing. Leg of Lamb with Roasted Garlic and Shallots, Chicken with Provençal Herbs and Garlic Potatoes, and Scallops with Tomatoes, Garlic, and Herbs are all good examples. Serve the main course with grains and simply garnished vegetables.

To moderate your cholesterol intake, choose dishes in which saturated fat can easily be replaced or eliminated. Use olive oil in place of butter when sautéing the mushrooms in Warm Salad of Wild Mushrooms. With Roast Sea Bass, use only olive oil in the Herb Butter Sauce, or omit the sauce altogether. In other recipes, fat, calories, and cholesterol can be further reduced by omitting some ingredients completely. Bacon, cream, and cheese all fall into this category.

Always consider the meal as a whole. Plan balanced menus using a healthy variety of fresh seasonal foods and cooking methods.

HOW-TO BOXES

In each of the recipes in **French Country Cooking** *you'll find pictures of all the techniques used. However, some basic preparations appear in a number of recipes, and these are shown in extra detail in these special "how-to" boxes:*

INDEX

ACKNOWLEDGMENTS

Photographers' Assistants Nick Allen and Sid Sideris

Chef Eric Treuille

Home Economist Maddalena Bastianelli

Typesetting Rowena Feeny and Axis Design

Text film by Disc to Print (UK) Limited

Production Consultant Lorraine Baird

*Carroll & Brown Limited would like to thank
Magimix (UK) Limited who supplied the
Cuisine Systeme food processor,
The Kitchenware Merchants Limited for
the Le Creuset cookware, and ICTC
(01603 488 019) for supplying the Cuisinox
Elysee pans used throughout the book*

*Anne Willan would like to thank her
chief editor Jacqueline Bobrow and
associate editor Valerie Cipollone for their
vital help with writing this book and
researching and testing the recipes, aided
by Brenda Garza, Karen Ryan, and
the La Varenne's chefs and trainees.*

Notes

• Metric and imperial measures have been calculated separately.
Only use one set of measures as they are not exact equivalents.

• All spoon measurements are level.

• Spoon measurements are calculated using a standard 5 ml teaspoon and
15 ml tablespoon to give an accurate measurement of small amounts.